FROM EXODUS TO EXILE

The Absolute Chronology Using Reconciled Data from Kings and Chronicles

John Ferris

Dedication

This book is for Crystal (Chris), the treasured mother of my children.

Acknowledgement

I want to extend my heartfelt gratitude to my friends and family for their unwavering encouragement throughout my journey of writing this book. Their valuable feedback and insightful questions illuminated key areas of inquiry.

I also wish to acknowledge the publisher who recognized the potential in my work and introduced me to talented professionals who profoundly elevated the final product. Even though most of them remain nameless to me, I deeply appreciate their contributions, feedback, and insights.

Contents

INTRODUCTION

The purpose of this book is to assess whether biblical scriptures can be regarded as a reliable historical record. With a strong inclination toward mathematics, I found the challenge of reconciling what often appears to be a chaotic mix of numbers especially compelling.

It is clear that there is a wealth of data and historical context available. During my career, I frequently dealt with complex financial scenarios involving numerous variables. This experience equipped me with transferable analytical skills, which I believe are well suited to navigating the intricacies of this subject.

Some commentators argue that the biblical references found in the Books of Kings and Chronicles are irreconcilable. This only fueled my curiosity further. The possibility of bringing clarity to what many consider an unsolvable puzzle became a motivating force, one that offered the satisfaction of achieving what others had deemed impossible.

Many biblical and historical scholars have attempted to untangle these complexities, employing a range of methods that vary from the insightful to the absurd. Two works that have garnered enduring attention are Ussher's *Annals of the World* (1650) and Thiele's *Mysterious Numbers of the Hebrew Kings* (1951). The supporters of these differing theories often fall into opposing camps, and it is widely acknowledged that both groups present arguments built on frameworks that contain significant flaws. Ultimately, this is not a matter of choosing one system over the other, it can be shown that both are fundamentally incorrect.

My objective is to reconcile conflicting viewpoints by thoroughly examining every available source of useful data, deciphering the complexity, and above all, uncovering the truth. Truth, after all, is far more fulfilling than defending a structure built on distortions or incomplete narratives. In this process, I aim to expose errors

1

and propose valid alternatives rooted in verifiable evidence and grounded reasoning.

The approach taken here will not be partisan. It is essential to remain unaffected by concerns over how the material presented might challenge established beliefs. This book will likely face scrutiny from skeptics and individuals with personal agendas, particularly those intent on discrediting conclusions that conflict with long-held views.

The goal is to construct a definitive chronology for the period under examination. However, before that can be credibly achieved, a number of significant errors, now deeply embedded in both academic and religious discourse, must be corrected. It is hoped that the new paradigm introduced here will inspire many moments of recognition and clarity.

It is important to clarify that the title of this book does not suggest that the starting point will be the Exodus. Instead, I will begin by establishing the most recent dates as fixed reference points and work backward to the earliest. The period of the Judges will fall outside the scope of this discussion.

CHAPTER 1

For nearly 1,850 years, curious minds have pursued the puzzle of the Old Testament kings, the rulers of Judah and Israel. While many scholars have confidently claimed to unlock the timeline, their conclusions often contradict each other and clash with broader biblical narratives. Yet despite the confusion, each theory finds loyal supporters, convinced they have uncovered the correct interpretation.

The earliest attempt to organize this chronology came from Rabbi Yose ben Halafta around 160 CE in his work, *Seder Olam Rabbah*. Although groundbreaking for its time, his effort largely reiterated what the Scriptures already provided. Later scholars, including Sextus Julius Africanus, Eusebius, and Bishop James Ussher, continued the quest to establish a biblical timeline. Still, the search for clarity remains an enduring source of debate and fascination.

To understand the broader events of the Second Millennium BCE, we must first establish reliable dates for the Divided Kingdom. Doing so requires abandoning outdated models that have left generations of researchers frustrated. As Einstein famously observed, "Sticking to the same approach and expecting different results is pure insanity." This study adopts a new, pragmatic approach, one that aims to move past the failures of previous methods and offer a clearer path forward. Let us now delve into this rich and complex historical puzzle.

The Thiele Chronology

In modern scholarship, Edwin R. Thiele (1895–1986) left a lasting mark with his influential book *The Mysterious Numbers of the Hebrew Kings*, first published in 1951 and revised in later editions through 1983. His chronology became a reference point for many historians attempting to date key events in the first half of the First Millennium BCE. However, Thiele's approach is not without its critics, largely due to significant weaknesses in his methodology.

B. S. Childs, in *Introduction to the Old Testament as Scripture* (Philadelphia: Fortress, 1979), p. 296, remarked:

"Thiele is forced to project innumerable coregencies, to reconstruct a complex interchange of calendars, and to rely on unique patterns of calculation… He has found few followers of his system apart from those who are committed apologetically to a doctrine of Scripture's absolute harmony." (Quoted in Tetley, 2005, p. 4)

A major flaw in Thiele's work was his reliance on the assumption that the Assyrian Eponym Lists and King Lists were entirely accurate. This allowed him to align biblical events with those recorded in Assyrian history, treating the Assyrian chronology as an authoritative benchmark.

Despite being a professing Christian and former Seventh Day Adventist missionary, Thiele placed greater confidence in the Assyrian records than in the biblical texts themselves. He stated:

"Between the absolute chronology of the Hebrews and that of their neighbours, there can be no conflict. If the Biblical chronology seems to be at variance with Assyrian chronology, it may be because of errors in the Hebrew records…" (Thiele, 1983, p. 4)

Thiele earned his PhD in biblical archaeology from the University of Chicago in 1943. He remained affiliated with Emmanuel Missionary College, which later became Andrews University in 1960. From 1963 to 1965, he served on the religion faculty as Professor of Antiquity. Today, Andrews University continues to draw archaeology students in part due to Thiele's enduring legacy.

Interestingly, the most ardent defenders of Thiele's chronology are almost always connected to that institution. In one particular exchange, a prominent commentator abruptly ended correspondence after it was suggested that his affiliation with

Andrews University might be influencing his unwavering support of Thiele's conclusions.

The Ussher Chronology:

Bishop Ussher's *Annals of the World*, first published in 1650, remains a fascinating work of historical reconstruction. Yet, in light of modern advancements, it is time to reevaluate its claims. Ussher's insights were impressive for his time, but many of his conclusions struggle under the scrutiny of contemporary geology, archaeology, and cosmology. These fields offer powerful tools that help us better understand both the biblical narrative and the world it seeks to describe.

Despite this, some still cling tightly to Ussher's chronology, often dismissing any evidence that challenges their beliefs. This resistance to new information can be perplexing. Jews and Christians alike share a long-standing tradition of interpreting Scripture in ways that evolve with the growth of knowledge. The prophet Daniel captured this ongoing journey when he wrote, *"But thou, O Daniel, shut up the words, and seal the book, even to the time of the end: many shall run to and fro, and knowledge shall be increased"* (Daniel 12:4).

We are fortunate to live in an era where knowledge has exploded. With every new discovery, we gain a more nuanced understanding of ancient events, including the chronology of the Divided Kingdom. Embracing this growing body of knowledge not only broadens our insight but also deepens our appreciation for the sacred texts that have shaped faith and culture for millennia.

Ussher's model, with its bold claim of identifying the exact moment of creation, has long stirred controversy. Those who question it often find themselves met with hostility, accused of denying the Word of God. But it is crucial to remember that *Annals of the World* is not part of the biblical canon. While Ussher's work is eloquent and historically significant, it is not infallible and does not carry the authority of Scripture itself. When subjected to modern academic standards, many of its conclusions begin to unravel.

To understand the context in which Ussher wrote, we must look at the intellectual climate of his time. Just before he published his chronology, the dominant view in the Church held that the Earth was the center of the universe. It was only in 1633 that Galileo was placed under house arrest for championing heliocentrism in his groundbreaking *Dialogue Concerning the Two Chief World Systems*. His defiance of religious orthodoxy marked a turning point in the clash between emerging science and entrenched dogma.

The stories of Ussher and Galileo remind us of the courage required to question prevailing beliefs. Throughout history, progress has often depended on those brave enough to challenge accepted truths. Embracing inquiry and healthy skepticism opens the door to deeper understanding and intellectual freedom.

Denialism

The term "denialism" often provokes strong reactions, and understandably so, it frequently points to deeper, uncomfortable realities. Consider Holocaust denial. Behind such revisionism lies a troubling mix of racial and religious prejudice that exposes more than just historical ignorance.

Similarly, for decades, tobacco companies denied the link between smoking and lung cancer. Their motivations were transparent: acknowledging the truth would lead to legal and financial consequences.

Even today, many people ignore the well-documented connection between diet and heart disease. Confronting this truth would require lifestyle changes that many find difficult or undesirable. In such cases, denial becomes a shield, a way to avoid facing uncomfortable facts.

Understanding denialism means recognizing the psychological and social forces that drive it. It challenges us to examine our own beliefs and consider what truths we might be unwilling to face.

As Hoofnagle (2007) explains:

"Denialism employs persuasive rhetorical tactics that create the illusion of a genuine debate, despite the absence of solid arguments. These misleading assertions thrive in environments where individuals lack substantial evidence to support their viewpoints, particularly when they stand in stark contradiction to established scientific consensus or overwhelming data. Such tactics successfully divert attention away from meaningful discussions by relying on emotionally charged yet ultimately hollow claims."

When it comes to reconstructing historical timelines, theories like those of Ussher and Thiele occupy a contentious and often polarizing space. Both offer frameworks that have sparked intense debate. However, when inconsistencies emerge or evidence contradicts their positions, proponents frequently retreat into rhetorical flourish or outright denialism rather than engaging in constructive dialogue.

Take the supporters of the Thiele position, for example. There can at times be an air of academic formality that may feel somewhat inaccessible or discouraging to some. They frequently employ intellectual sleight of hand, crafting narratives that may appear polished but crumble under closer examination. Conversely, the Ussher camp tends to lean on obfuscation as a defense mechanism, muddying the waters of interpretation until even questionable claims begin to sound plausible.

What's particularly fascinating is how both camps respond when confronted with archaeological, mathematical, or scientific evidence that contradicts their conclusions. Ussherites, in particular, often dismiss entire disciplines outright. Rather than engage with the evidence, they may selectively distort or cherry-pick data to reinforce their predetermined views. This is a hallmark of denialism, a strategy that trades inquiry for dogma.

Regardless of how courteously these arguments are presented, both factions demonstrate a troubling tendency toward denialism. This refusal to engage openly with contradictory evidence undermines honest discourse and hinders the search for historical truth. At some point, we must ask ourselves: when will we choose evidence over rhetoric in our pursuit of understanding?

Issues with the Ussher and Thiele Models

The **Ussher** and **Thiele** chronologies are two well-known systems for dating events in the Bible, especially the Old Testament. Each has its own framework and assumptions, and both have drawn criticism from scholars for different reasons. Both the Ussher and Thiele models attempt to construct a precise biblical chronology, but they falter in key areas. While they often present themselves as definitive guides, their frameworks rest on assumptions that clash with established Jewish literature, especially texts like the Mishnah and the Tractate Rosh Hashanah.

Take, for instance, an insightful scenario described in the Mishnah. It recounts a case in which a new king, though the son of a recently deceased monarch, ascends to the throne in the month of Nisan after being elected in Adar, the final month of the year. Intuitively, one might think that his reign would begin immediately, and that Nisan would mark the start of his second year. But Rabbi Johanan clarifies otherwise. R. Hisda further explains that the Mishnah's rule, that a king's year is counted from Nisan, applies only to the kings of Israel. For foreign rulers, the count begins in Tishri.

This distinction illustrates a nuanced timekeeping method known as the "accession year" or "postdating" system. Under this method, a king's first official year begins with the start of the calendar year following his accession. In contrast, the "non-accession" or "antedating" system counts even a partial year as the king's first. This practice was common among neighboring nations but was not the standard in ancient Israel or Judah.

By examining these divergent methods of reckoning royal reigns, we gain deeper insight into the ancient world and the profound importance attached to time, leadership, and record-keeping. These subtleties are essential to constructing an accurate chronology.

The implications of these distinctions are significant. While scholars like Ussher and Thiele often claim fidelity to Scripture, their methodologies can overlook critical contextual details preserved in Jewish tradition. Such oversights risk distorting the broader narrative and timeline of Israel's rich and complex history.

To truly understand these ancient records, we must move beyond simplified models and engage with the authoritative teachings embedded in centuries of Jewish scholarship. The biblical texts are not just theological or literary artifacts; they are repositories of intricate numerical and historical data. When we interpret that data through the lens of enduring rabbinical wisdom, we open the door to a far more accurate and meaningful grasp of biblical events.

Accession and non-accession use by Ussher and Thiele:

Larry Pierce, a passionate advocate of the Ussher model delves deep into the complex timeline of *The Annals of the World*. In his analysis, he outlines two distinct systems used to calculate the chronology of the Divided Kingdom.

According to Pierce, the Northern Kingdom (NK), representing Israel, initially adopted the Non-Accession Year system during Jeroboam's reign. This system persisted through the reigns of eight kings, from Jeroboam to Ahaziah. After Ahaziah, however, the kingdom transitioned to the Accession Year system, a method traditionally used in the Southern Kingdom (SK), Judah. This change appears with Jehoram, who adopted Judah's calendrical approach.

Interestingly, Pierce notes that Ussher speculated Amaziah may have also used the Accession Year system, asserting that the biblical text supports either method. Ahab had appointed his son Amaziah as viceroy, and Pierce suggests this transition likely occurred during the Jewish New Year, further highlighting the relevance of the Accession system to his reign.

Shifting focus, Edwin Thiele observed that the Non-Accession Year system surfaced only once in the Southern Kingdom, during the reign of Joash. This introduces a key point of divergence. Ussher, despite his thorough work, overlooked a crucial detail: Israel counted its year from 1 Nisan (the first month) to the end of Adar I, or Adar II in leap years, whereas Judah's year began on 1 Tishri (the seventh month) and ended with the last day of Elul (the sixth month). Thiele acknowledged the six-month gap between Israel and Judah's New Year celebrations but failed to incorporate this discrepancy into his calculations. This oversight presents one of several significant flaws in Ussher's chronology and invites deeper scrutiny into biblical timelines.

The Belgian priest and scholar Valerius Josephus Coucke (2 February 1888 – 20 December 1951) revolutionized our understanding of ancient calendars in the early 20th century. He revealed that Israel's calendar began in Nisan, just as spring renewed the earth, while Judah's year commenced in Tishri, aligning with the autumn harvest.

But here's the twist: Jesuit priest and mathematician Franz Xaver Kugler (27 November 1862 – 25 January 1929) made the discovery independently years earlier.

Despite these discoveries, many followers of Ussher remain resolute in their belief that both kingdoms began their years in Nisan. This misconception traces back to the 17th century, when Ussher assembled *The Annals*. Had he known of the Nisan–Tishri split, it's hard to imagine he wouldn't have revised his conclusions. Yet, modern adherents cling to his interpretations, treating them as immutable truths, even in the face of compelling contrary evidence.

Then comes Thiele's intriguing methodology. He employed both accession and non-accession systems in his calculations for the Hebrew kings' reigns.

He explained:

"In the non-accession-year system, the first official year of a ruler is counted as the last year of the previous one, leading to some pretty complex calculations." *(Thiele, 1983:13)*

Thiele's exploration of biblical chronology is both fascinating and fraught with controversy. While he reached conclusions similar to those of Kugler and Coucke, his unwillingness to adopt newer insights kept him tethered to outdated interpretations. Like Ussher, Thiele employed a clever tactic: by selectively using the non-accession system, he could mold the figures to fit a predetermined narrative.

Imagine the power to add or subtract years at will.

Though this manipulation ran counter to Talmudic principles, it served as a powerful tool, allowing both Ussher and Thiele to align their timelines with scripture while subtly reinforcing their own theological agendas. In doing so, they preserved their narrative frameworks but obscured historical accuracy.

How did Ussher and Thiele arrive at their dates?

These two scholars, deeply invested in the timeline of biblical events, arrived at strikingly different conclusions. Despite referencing the same ancient texts, their interpretations diverged sharply.

On one side stands Ussher, who placed the beginning of the Divided Kingdom at 975 BCE. On the other, Thiele arrived at 931/930 BCE. A 45-year discrepancy is an unacceptable gap in such a meticulously studied chronology.

As we progress, it will become evident that the accurate date lies somewhere between their two estimates.

Ussher's Method:

James Ussher, a diligent student of biblical history, turned to Ezekiel 4:4–5 for guidance. These verses, often cited for their symbolic weight, read:

"Lie thou also upon thy left side, and lay the iniquity of the house of Israel upon it:

According to the number of the days that thou shalt lie upon it, thou shalt bear their iniquity.

For I have laid upon thee the years of their iniquity, according to the number of the days,

Three hundred and ninety days: so shalt thou bear the iniquity of the house of Israel." *(KJV)*

Ezekiel adds another 40 days in verse six, interpreting them as years to account for the sins of Judah. From this intricate calculation, Ussher determined that the 390 years representing Israel's transgressions concluded in 586 BCE, the pivotal year when Judah fell to the Babylonians and was exiled.

"What Ezekiel 4 reinforces, rather than introduces, is the distinction between Israel and Judah as separate entities, a theme already clear throughout the Books of Kings and Chronicles. In this case, Ezekiel underscores it through the unequal periods of judgment: 390 years for Israel's sins and 40 for Judah's." Although Ussher's calculation of 390 years before 586 BCE was not based on 390 full calendar years, but rather on 388 complete years plus two partial years, and it led him to propose 975 BCE as the starting point.

With this framework in place, Ussher fit the reigns of Israel and Judah into his timeline. This was no simple task, it required him to introduce two interregnum periods totaling 21 years: one lasting 9 years, the other 12. Yet this book challenges that notion, arguing that no such interregnum periods occurred.

Critique: The Enigmatic Chronology of Israel

The story of ancient Israel is steeped in mystery and contradiction, a narrative inviting us to peel back the layers of sacred history. The northern kingdom was absorbed by the Assyrian Empire in 722 BCE. If we accept Ussher's proposed starting point of 975 BCE, Israel's national life spanned just 253 years. That's a blink of an eye compared to the 390 days/years stated in Ezekiel 4, relating to the sins of Israel.

This discrepancy is not a trivial footnote, it exposes deep inconsistencies in Ussher's chronology. It suggests that revisiting Scripture with a critical lens is not just helpful, it's essential.

As we turn to the Scriptures, the contrasts between the Septuagint (LXX) and the Masoretic Text reveal a web of contradictions. Take Ezekiel 4:4–6, where God issues an extraordinary command:

"And thou shalt lie upon thy left side, and lay the iniquities of the house of Israel upon it... For I have appointed thee their iniquities for a number of days, for a hundred and ninety days: so shalt thou bear the iniquities of the house of Israel..."

The paradox is clear. While translations vary, one conclusion is unmistakable: Israel's 190 days/years, plus Judah's 40 days/years, total 230 days/years. Strikingly, later revelations in this book will align with that very number, suggesting that divided Israel existed from 952 BCE to 722 BCE, a span of exactly 230 years.

But what of the 390 days/years in the Hebrew texts? That number often feels like a later interpolation, an outlier that even raised the eyebrows of Saint Jerome (c. 347–420). In his time, the shorter 190-day span was more widely recognized. The longstanding tendency of commentators, Ussher included, to cherry-pick data while avoiding the tension—real or perceived—between figures in Kings and Chronicles. In reality, these texts are largely harmonious, with only minor, non-impactful discrepancies. The primary distinction lies in their purpose: one historical, the other theological and restorative."

Solving this chronological enigma demands more than arithmetic, it requires dissecting over seventy distinct data points scattered across the texts. This daunting task eluded even the analytical minds of Ussher and Thiele. Yet it remains vital for any serious student of Israel's past. The challenge is laid before us: can we untangle the threads to uncover the authentic narrative?

Thiele: A Chronicle of Confidence and Conjecture

Edwin R. Thiele's unwavering belief in the accuracy of the Assyrian records guided his work. His goal: to align biblical events with Assyrian chronology. This pursuit was shaped by his academic journey, earning an MA in Archaeology in 1937 and a PhD in Biblical Archaeology from the University of Chicago in 1943.

But Thiele's commitment to Assyrian data came at a cost. What began as academic rigour often morphed into a fragile balancing act, one marked by conjecture, circular reasoning, and questionable assumptions. In his attempt to shoehorn biblical events into the Assyrian timeline, Thiele often lost sight of the complexities and tensions inherent in the biblical record.

The result? A chronology that is less a coherent narrative and more a mosaic of selective harmonizations, convincing on the surface, but riddled with underexamined flaws.

A Warning Ignored: The Voice of Luckenbill

Nearly a century ago, historian Daniel Luckenbill offered a caution that still echoes today:

"One soon discovers that the accurate portrayal of events as they took place, year by year during the [Assyrian] king's reign, was not the guiding motive of the royal scribes."

This insight is a sober reminder: history, especially royal history, is often shaded by vanity and personal agenda. It is not the neutral record many assume it to be.

Yet Thiele, in *The Mysterious Numbers of the Hebrew Kings (MNHK)*, references Luckenbill more than twenty times, without heeding this very warning. This oversight undermines the credibility of Thiele's conclusions and calls into question the foundation of his reconstructed timeline.

An Invitation to Reconsider

As students of history, we are called not just to absorb facts, but to question them. The Assyrian timeline is not just a ledger of kings, it's a crafted narrative, rich in ambition and embellishment.

If we are to approach biblical chronology with integrity, we must challenge inherited assumptions, reevaluate long-held interpretations, and remain open to mystery. Only then can we begin to see the ancient story of Israel not as a resolved equation, but as a living puzzle, waiting to be faithfully unraveled.

Revised Version:

Edwin Thiele's *Mysterious Numbers of the Hebrew Kings* (MNHK) generated considerable excitement when he claimed it was entirely aligned with Scripture. However, a deeper examination of his assertions reveals a different story, one that raises more questions than it answers. Let us consider several revealing quotes from Thiele himself.

He opens with a bold proclamation:

"The Assyrian system provided us with an absolute chronology, fixed by modern astronomical calculations."

Yet, in the same breath, he portrays the Hebrew chroniclers as somehow "inferior," suggesting they had borrowed from their more advanced Assyrian neighbors (Thiele, 1983, p. 27).

As the text unfolds, Thiele acknowledges the difficulty in harmonizing the biblical and Assyrian timelines:

"...there seems to be a wide divergence between biblical and established Assyrian datings for the same events" (p. 38).

He continues by candidly admitting:

"The Israelitish numbers and the parallel numbers referring to Judah do not agree" (p. 41).

Despite these conflicts, Thiele maintains an almost unshakable trust in Assyrian chronology:

"Assyrian chronology back to the beginning of the ninth century B.C. rests on a highly dependable basis" (p. 67).

His confidence culminates in an astonishing assertion:

"Any date in Hebrew history that might synchronize with an absolute date in Assyrian history would have to be correct" (p. 139).

This juxtaposition is both fascinating and troubling. Thiele elevates the Assyrian record to near-infallibility, while casting doubt on the coherence of the Hebrew accounts. The result is a pattern that reflects a clear imbalance, a preferential bias that colors his analysis.

As we sift through Thiele's claims, what emerges is a whirlwind of scholarly ambition clouded by selective reasoning. His pursuit of a harmonized timeline between Assyrian and Hebrew narratives flirts with hyperbole, raising crucial questions about the cost of such forced synchronization. Are we uncovering truth, or crafting a version of history that fits too neatly?

One particularly revealing moment comes when Thiele claims that modern astronomical calculations have firmly anchored the Assyrian chronology (p. 27). Yet, it isn't until nearly fifty pages later that he provides any real substantiation. He briefly references *The Almagest*, noting that it records over eighty astronomical positions, solar, lunar, and planetary, which modern astronomers have verified.

Among these, he highlights a solar eclipse that occurred during the first year of Mardokempados, also known as Merodach-baladan. According to Thiele, this eclipse began in Babylon just an hour after moonrise and was total, a rare and impressive event, dated to March 19, 721 BCE (p. 71).

However, the two centuries preceding this eclipse, spanning much of the Divided Kingdom era, lack any comparable, verifiable astronomical data. And that period, from roughly 952 BCE to 722 BCE, witnessed seismic events, including the fall of the Northern Kingdom (Samaria) and the dispersion of its people into the Assyrian Empire.

Thiele offers no astronomical evidence to confirm any specific dates within this crucial span. The lone exception is the Bur-Sagale solar eclipse, not mentioned in *The Almagest*, which darkened the skies on June 15, 763 BCE and is recorded in the Assyrian annals as occurring during the ninth year of King Ashur-dan III. Notably, *The Almagest* only references dates from 747 BCE onward, making the Bur-Sagale eclipse, which predates it, an outlier.

This context invites serious scrutiny. If Thiele's assertions were as robust as he implies, why does he delay in presenting his key evidence? Why are his arguments supported by a single eclipse, with a 200-year vacuum before it? The inconsistencies weaken the structural integrity of his thesis and expose a deeper issue: a persistent bias toward the Assyrian historical narrative, often at the expense of the Hebrew record.

In the captivating field of ancient astronomy, *The Almagest* stands as a monumental work, chronicling nearly one hundred precisely dated observations. Of particular interest are the Babylonian records of three lunar eclipses from 721 BCE. Ptolemy, the famed Greco-Roman astronomer, highlighted these events as the earliest definitive accounts, despite having access to even older Babylonian data.

This tidbit raises eyebrows when considering Thiele's argument that Assyrian chronology finds validation in Ptolemy's *Almagest*. Upon closer examination, the claim begins to falter. The overlap between reliable astronomical data and the historical records of the Assyrians and Hebrews spans from 721 BCE to the early 6th century BCE, during the Babylonian exile. While most historians generally agree on this timeline, Thiele's interpretation, particularly concerning the reign of Sennacherib, remains problematic. In this case, the much-touted astronomical evidence fails to bring clarity.

How Ussher and Thiele Dealt with the Problem of 2 Kings 15:1 and 2

A curious puzzle emerges in the intricate world of biblical chronology: "In the twenty-seventh year of Jeroboam, king of Israel, Azariah, son of Amaziah, began to reign as king of Judah" (2 Kings 15:1). The twenty-seventh year of Jeroboam corresponds to 777 BCE.

"He was sixteen years old when he became king ..." (2 Kings 15:2a). Uzziah was crowned king in 789 BCE upon the death of Amaziah.

These seemingly straightforward verses have provoked considerable debate among historians, chronologists, and theologians. Scholars like James Ussher and Edwin Thiele have attempted, each in their own way, to solve the chronological tangle resulting from the conflation of events separated by twelve years.

At first glance, the issue appears simple. But as one digs deeper, it quickly becomes a labyrinth of competing theories and interpretations. Let's explore the explanations offered by these brilliant minds and how they attempted to make sense of this historical enigma.

Take Ussher, for example. He speculated:

"Jeroboam II seems to have been made viceroy of the kingdom by his father, Joash."

This suggests a political structure that included shared rule, perhaps to ensure stability during turbulent times. Ussher expanded his theory:

"Uzziah, or Azariah, succeeded him [Amaziah] in the 27th year of Jeroboam, king of Israel, reckoning from the time that he began to reign as co-regent with his father [Jehoash]."

Here, Ussher constructs a picture of interwoven regencies, family dynamics, and legacy.

But history seldom offers neat transitions. Ussher highlights the upheaval following Jeroboam's death:

"When Jeroboam died, the kingdom seriously declined."

The resulting chaos led to a period of intense instability, a staggering eleven and a half years of leaderless disorder in Israel. Ussher factored this interregnum into his timeline, but in doing so, he misunderstood the scriptural context. This misreading introduced a significant error.

In Judah's parallel narrative, the reigns of Amaziah and Jeroboam II intersect in ways that have confounded many. Ussher made a common mistake: he assumed that Amaziah died in the 27th year of Jeroboam II. This assumption led him to propose a speculative twelve-year coregency between Jeroboam and his father,

Jehoash, along with an eleven-and-a-half-year gap at the end of Jeroboam's reign. The current research presented in this book challenges these assumptions, casting doubt on Ussher's reconstruction.

Thiele, despite his scholarly precision, fell into a similar chronological trap. According to 2 Kings 14:23, Jeroboam II reigned for forty-one years. Thiele argued that Jeroboam died fourteen years after Amaziah's reign, but this conclusion rested on a critical twelve-year miscalculation. In truth, Jeroboam II died in the 38th year of Azariah's (Uzziah's) rule, which also marks the beginning of Zechariah's six-month reign (2 Kings 15:8). This discrepancy ripples through Thiele's timeline, creating confusion that is difficult to unravel without consulting a detailed chart provided in this volume.

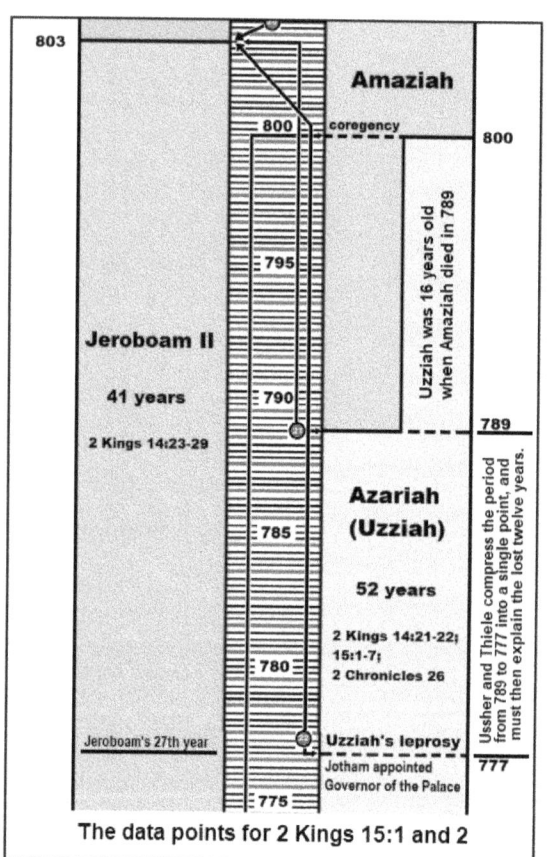

The data points for 2 Kings 15:1 and 2

Like Ussher, Thiele noted that a significant shift occurred when Amaziah launched a bold, yet ultimately disastrous, military campaign against Israel. Jehoash captured him, creating a power vacuum in Judah. In response, the people appointed young Azariah (Uzziah), only sixteen at the time, as their new king (2 Kings 14:21).

However, this account is flawed.

In truth, Azariah's accession as coregent did not result from Amaziah's downfall. It occurred eleven years before his father's death, when Azariah was just five years old. The military disaster at the hands of Jehoash did not cause Azariah's rise; rather, it was an earlier strategic decision. The campaign that led to Amaziah's capture (vv. 8–14) marked a turning point, but not the beginning of Azariah's reign.

Conclusion

The saga of Ussher and Thiele converges at a critical historical bottleneck: the overlapping reigns of Azariah and Amaziah. This conundrum lies at the heart of the complexities facing anyone attempting to nail down precise biblical chronologies. The attempt to reconcile these conflicting data points illustrates the broader challenges inherent in interpreting ancient texts, especially when modern expectations of precision collide with ancient narrative conventions.

In the end, their efforts reveal not only the difficulty of aligning biblical timelines but also the intellectual rigor, and occasional overreach, involved in trying to make the pieces fit.

An Unexpected Tangent

Let us dive into an intriguing historical moment captured in the Bible, specifically in the second book of Kings:

"In the twenty-seventh year of Jeroboam, king of Israel, began Azariah, son of Amaziah, king of Judah, to reign. Sixteen years old was he when he began to reign, and he reigned fifty-two years in Jerusalem…" *2 Kings 15:1–2*

At first glance, this passage appears straightforward. It seems to tell us that young Azariah, also known as Uzziah, began his rule at the age of sixteen, during the 27th year of Jeroboam II's reign. However, upon closer inspection, this narrative contains subtle complexities. The editors of the Books of Kings have placed these verses in proximity, yet they refer to **two distinct events**: Azariah's initial assumption of kingship at sixteen and, twelve years later, his transition to a reign marked by his leprosy, during which his son Jotham conveyed royal directives on his behalf.

Here's where it gets fascinating.

While Azariah indeed ascended the throne at sixteen, many historical interpretations suggest he did so following his father Amaziah's death, possibly in the **15th year** of Jeroboam II's rule. Then, **twelve years later**, in Jeroboam's 27th year, Azariah, now 28, is said to have "begun to reign" again.

How can this be?

To unravel the mystery, we must appreciate the biblical use of the phrase **"began to reign."** It does not always signify the start of a sole reign. Rather, it can represent a significant shift in status, whether from vice-regency to co-regency or even a transformation due to personal or political crises. In Azariah's case, that transformation was tragic. Once a prominent king, he transgressed by burning incense in the Temple, an act reserved for priests. As punishment, he was struck with leprosy. This affliction isolated him from his people, the Temple, and even his palace.

Thus, the second "begin to reign" in the 27th year of Jeroboam wasn't the start of a reign in power, but a **change**, a reign in **quarantine**. Azariah governed from a distance while Jotham assumed executive authority.

This peculiar twelve-year gap between two reign markers isn't unique.

In fact, the Books of Kings use the phrase "began to reign" about **forty times**, each denoting pivotal shifts in royal authority. While these mentions tend to be clear and singular for the kings of Israel, the reigns of **Judean kings** often show greater temporal complexity. There are at least six cases, Ahaziah, Azariah, Jotham, Ahaz, Hezekiah, and Jehoiachin, where the phrase is used **twice** for the same king, reflecting distinct political or personal transitions.

Thiele's chronological methodology does recognize these dual references but consistently consolidates them into a single reign date, assuming overlapping scribal traditions. Yet the evidence points to a far more complex reality. While Thiele occasionally compressed timelines by a year or two in five cases, he dramatically expanded Azariah's eleven-year coregency with his father Amaziah to twenty-four years—an insertion of thirteen extra years. Simultaneously, he posited a twelve-year coregency between Jehoash and Jeroboam II of Israel. Taken together, these adjustments amount to a cumulative compression and expansion of twenty-one years, a substantial error in his chronological reconstruction. Much of this can be attributed to his treatment of so-called "dual-dating," which he interprets as two references to the same point in time, but the evidence suggests that this approach has led to significant chronological distortions. This oversight reemerges later in the sequence and also puzzled scholars like James Ussher. Ussher attempted to reconcile the anomaly by postulating a twelve-year **interregnum**, a throne left vacant between rulers.

Now consider another compelling case: **Ahaziah of Judah.**

Two seemingly contradictory accounts appear in scripture:

"In the twelfth year of Joram the son of Ahab king of Israel did Ahaziah the son of Jehoram king of Judah begin to reign." *2 Kings 8:25*

"And in the eleventh year of Joram the son of Ahab began Ahaziah to reign over Judah." *2 Kings 9:29*

These overlapping entries have stirred considerable scholarly debate. Thiele (1983:54) explored the possibility that the conflict arises from differing **chronological systems**.

He proposed a scenario involving **two scribes**, each adhering to a different reckoning method. One used the **accession-year system**, marking Ahaziah's reign in Joram's **eleventh year**. The other used the **non-accession-year method**, placing it in Joram's **twelfth year**. This kind of discrepancy speaks to the broader complexity of ancient Near Eastern chronography, and this book offers a **definitive solution** to this mystery.

Adding another layer of intrigue, the timing of Ahaziah's death might also explain the variance. If he died in the Hebrew month of Tishri—shortly after his coronation following his father's death—he would not be credited with a second regnal year. This would allow Athaliah, his mother, to claim that year as her own. (Coronations could occur any time during the first month, or even at the start of the second.)

The very title of Thiele's work, *The Mysterious Numbers of the Hebrew Kings*, is well chosen. It captures the persistent **confusion** that envelops these ancient timelines.

Jotham of Judah

Jotham, the son of Uzziah, became king of Judah at twenty-five, amid growing political unrest under **Pekah** of Israel. He reigned in Jerusalem for sixteen years, navigating through internal and external challenges.

But Jotham's rise was not without complexity.

For the majority of Uzziah's reign, after he became a leper at age 28 and was required by law to live in isolation, his son Jotham functioned as a vice-regent, effectively carrying out the king's duties and exercising full authority. The biblical record confirms this arrangement:

"Jotham the king's son was over the house, judging the people of the land." *2 Kings 15:5*

This transitional leadership prepared Jotham for the crown. Uzziah had reigned for fifty-two years, suggesting he likely died around the age of fifty-seven. The vice-regency thus allowed for a smoother shift in power, one rooted in **continuity** rather than chaos.

In a time when kings often assumed power at a young age, royal families prioritized early heirs. With multiple wives, kings frequently fathered children in their teenage years. This tradition places Jotham, a historically significant figure, at just twelve years old when he likely became Governor of the Palace.

Operating under the shadow of his father Uzziah's reign, marked by both triumph and turmoil, Jotham quickly emerged as a key figure. By age twenty-five, he was already serving as vice-regent, wielding authority beyond what his title typically implied. As years passed, his influence grew. Before Uzziah officially stepped down, Jotham was elevated to the position of coregent. Eventually, at age forty-one, he assumed full kingship in his own right.

But what of the intriguing overlap between Jotham and Jeroboam II?

At twenty-five, Jotham stepped into power during the closing years of Jeroboam II's impressive forty-one-year reign. This overlapping period invites closer scrutiny. A compelling reference in *2 Chronicles* affirms the concurrent leadership: **"Genealogies reckoned all these in the days of Jotham king of Judah and in the days of Jeroboam king of Israel"** (2 Chron. 5:17).

This synchronism raises questions, especially when examined alongside the contrasting chronologies of scholars like James Ussher and Edwin Thiele. Thiele's reconstruction places Jeroboam II's reign from 782 to 753 BCE, with Uzziah's leprosy emerging in 751/750 BCE, two years after Jeroboam's death. Under this timeline, Jotham would not have held any royal title during Jeroboam's lifetime.

Ussher, however, presents a different narrative. He argues that during Uzziah's seclusion due to leprosy, Jotham presided over the palace and administered governance. According to Ussher:

"When Jeroboam died, Jotham had not yet been born" (Ussher, 1650: ref. 564).

This conclusion suggests that Jotham's dual mentions of beginning his reign reflect entirely separate phases in his political ascent.

Such exploration highlights the recurring challenge in biblical chronology: determining whether recorded ages signify a king's vice-regency, coregency, or sole reign. While some, like Hezekiah, are measured strictly from their solo kingship, others reflect overlapping roles, poorly documented yet deeply significant.

Ahaz

The two verses that mark the beginning of Ahaz's reign are:

"In the seventeenth year of Pekah, son of Remaliah, Ahaz, son of Jotham, king of Judah, began to reign. Ahaz was twenty years old when he ascended the throne and reigned for sixteen years in Jerusalem…" (2 Kings 16:1–2).

Upon examination, it becomes clear that the seventeenth year of Pekah signifies the moment Ahaz deposed his father, Jotham, after an eight-year coregency. Jotham's own reign, initiated following Uzziah's departure, had begun seven years earlier.

Mathematical and biological clues support this theory. It's plausible that Ahaz was appointed vice-regent at twenty, likely around the same time Jotham began his independent rule. At Uzziah's abdication, Jotham was approximately forty years old, a realistic age for having a twenty-year-old son.

This timeline aligns closely with Ussher's interpretation: **"Tremellius [Immanuel Tremellius, c. 1510–1580] interprets that Ahaz was not twenty years old at the beginning of his reign, but rather when his father Jotham began his reign"** (Ussher, 1650: ref. 579).

At the time of Ahaz's death, he would have been 42 or 43. His son Hezekiah was twenty-five (2 Kings 18:2), which places Ahaz's age at fatherhood around seventeen or eighteen. This contrasts sharply with the traditional interpretation that has him becoming a father at eleven.

The stronger likelihood is that the two instances in which Ahaz "began to reign" represent separate milestones: his appointment as vice-regent and his eventual rise to sole kingship.

Hezekiah

The scriptural account of Hezekiah's reign begins with:

"Now it came to pass in the third year of Hoshea, son of Elah, king of Israel, that Hezekiah, the son of Ahaz, king of Judah, began to reign. He was twenty-five years old when he ascended the throne, and he reigned for twenty-nine years in Jerusalem..." (2 Kings 18:1–2).

The language here points to two distinct events: the first marking Hezekiah's appointment as coregent, and the second as his formal enthronement as sole king. Further evidence includes four additional examples of similar dual synchronisms in the biblical record. These reinforce the notion that Hezekiah's full kingship began when he was twenty-five, but his political role started earlier.

Jehoiachin

The examination of two biblical passages concerning the beginning of Jehoiachin's reign presents a longstanding scholarly puzzle:

"Jehoiachin was eighteen years old when he began to reign, and he reigned in Jerusalem three months..." *(2 Kings 24:8)*

"Jehoiachin was eight years old when he began to reign, and he reigned three months and ten days in Jerusalem..." *(2 Chronicles 36:9)*

This apparent discrepancy has often been cited as evidence of either a textual contradiction or a potential scribal error.

However, when applying the conventions of royal succession in the kingdom of Judah, a more nuanced interpretation emerges. One possibility is that Jehoiachin was appointed as a vice-regent or coregent at the age of eight and later ascended to full kingship at eighteen, following his father's death. Yet this interpretation faces a major obstacle: if he had indeed served as coregent starting at age eight, the years of his joint rule would typically be counted in the total length of his reign. However, the biblical record gives his reign as lasting only a few months—enough, by the usual reckoning, to claim a full regnal year, making his total reign effectively eleven years.

Given this inconsistency, the most plausible explanation is a scribal error. Whether Jehoiachin was eight or eighteen at the time of his ascension does not drastically alter the sequence of events surrounding his short-lived rule. However, historical context strengthens the case for the latter. Jehoiachin was installed as king upon the death of his father, and became a vassal king under Nebuchadnezzar of Babylon, a position that would almost certainly have required a ruler of sufficient age and maturity. Installing an eight-year-old in such a politically sensitive role would have been improbable.

Azariah / Uzziah

Turning to Azariah, also known as Uzziah, reveals deeper structural flaws in the interpretive model proposed by Edwin Thiele. His chronology appears constrained by a rigid framework that, rather than illuminating the biblical timeline, often obscures it with layered assumptions and questionable synchronisms.

Thiele's reconstructions rely on the premise that Azariah's accession must align with a calculated date, 767 BCE, coinciding with the twenty-seventh year of

Jeroboam II's reign. He writes:

"The twenty-nine years of Amaziah terminate in 767, the twenty-seventh year of Jeroboam II, which is the synchronism of Azariah's accession. Thus, if 767 is indeed established as the twenty-seventh year of Jeroboam II, and considering that Jehoash died merely fifteen years prior, it follows that Jeroboam II must have ruled for twelve years before his father's demise." *(Thiele, 1983:111)*

This line of reasoning rests on a precarious foundation. To support the supposed synchronism between Amaziah's death and Jeroboam II's 27th year, Thiele proposes an unverified twelve-year coregency between Jehoash and Jeroboam. But this move raises more problems than it solves.

Rather than clarify the timeline, Thiele's approach introduces a twelve-year gap into Israel's chronology, one that lacks direct scriptural support. This is not the only instance of such a significant error. To create a synchronicity between Tiglath-pileser III and Menahem, Thiele has altered the order of reigns in 2 *Kings 17 and 18*, pushing Menahem's reign back by eleven years, and indulging in historical revisionism with the latter Israelite reigns.

A simpler, more textually faithful interpretation would bypass the need for such speculative coregencies altogether. In seeking to resolve one difficulty, Thiele ends up entangling the narrative in a web of unnecessary complications.

Conclusion

Imagine reading a rich historical narrative only to be confronted by six puzzling apparent contradictions likely introduced not by the original authors, but by later editors attempting to streamline complex data. Instead of offering clarity, these editorial interventions created ambiguity, transforming minor discrepancies into full-blown paradoxes. Untangling these knots has demanded not only scholarly rigor but also immense patience and interpretive care.

In the end, while textual anomalies persist, careful contextual analysis often reveals simpler explanations. By revisiting assumptions and honoring the integrity of the source material, we move closer to understanding the historical truths embedded within the biblical record.

CHAPTER 2

The two records concerning Amaziah and Uzziah describe events that occurred twelve years apart. Since there was no joint rule between Jehoash and Jeroboam II, it becomes clear that Amaziah died and his son Azariah, also known as Uzziah, became king during the fifteenth year of Jeroboam II's reign.

This moment marked a significant shift, not only in Uzziah's ascent but in the structure of governance in the Kingdom of Judah. To understand why a king from that period might appear to "begin to reign" more than once, we must examine the various modes of ruling that existed in Israel and Judah.

There are six distinct forms of reign. This book uses terminology consistent with historical norms but substitutes the term "viceroy" with "vice-regent" for clarity. Below is a detailed explanation of each form to enhance our understanding.

Vice-Regent

This title was bestowed upon the king's eldest son, identifying him as the designated heir to the throne. Most heirs held this prestigious position at some point in their lives, though the Scriptures rarely document such appointments.

While the position signified great honor, the vice-regent's power was limited. His authority stemmed from the king's mandate, allowing him to act with the full weight of his father's rule in specific matters. The title "Vice-Regent" was effectively synonymous with "King," as no distinct Hebrew term exists for vice-regent or coregent.

It's important to note that vice-regents were not counted as reigning monarchs in official records. However, their tenure is often critical for understanding succession and timeline alignment.

Also, "Vice-Regent" should not be confused with "Viceroy," which refers to a royal representative residing in a foreign land on behalf of the king.

Coregency

A coregency was a unique political arrangement used as a preemptive strategy when a reigning monarch perceived a threat to their rule, be it military defeat, serious illness, or old age. By appointing a coregent, the king ensured a stable transition in the event of sudden death.

In theory, both the reigning monarch and the coregent shared equal authority. The coregent bore the same royal title and participated in ruling the kingdom. Still, in practice, many kings retained dominant control until the very end of their lives.

Unlike vice-regents, coregents were officially recognized, and their years of shared rule were included in the total length of a king's reign. This formal acknowledgment solidified their legitimacy and fostered continuity, which was vital for national stability.

Sole Reign

A sole reign began with the death of the previous king. While the new monarch was recognized immediately, the official regnal count did not start until the first day of the new year, Nisan in Israel and Tishri in Judah.

Any coregency at the start or end of the king's reign was included in his total years of rule. If a king died after the first month of his final regnal year, that year was counted. The period before his official inauguration was termed the "Zero Year."

Abdication

Historical records suggest four notable cases of abdication in Judah and Israel. Typically, abdication occurred when illness left a king unable to rule effectively. In such cases, a coregent, often the king's son, was appointed and granted full royal authority, while the former king retained his title.

A remarkable exception is King Jehoshaphat, who abdicated while still healthy and died two years later (2 Kings 8:16). This voluntary abdication represents a deviation from customary practice and illustrates the complexities of royal transitions. Three other cases of abdication exist but remain obscure and largely unacknowledged.

Deposition

In rare instances, a reigning monarch was forcibly removed. King Jotham, for example, was deposed by his son Ahaz after a 16-year reign. Though he continued to live for at least four more years, he held no power during that time.

2 Kings 15:30 reflects the political instability of that era:

"And Hoshea the son of Elah made a conspiracy against Pekah the son of Remaliah, and struck him and killed him, and reigned in his stead, in the twentieth year of Jotham the son of Uzziah."

This passage suggests overlapping timelines and the political fluidity that characterized transitions of power.

Appointment

Following King Josiah's unexpected defeat by Pharaoh Necho II of Egypt, the political climate in Judah underwent a dramatic transformation. Once independent and prosperous, the kingdom fell under Egyptian control.

This period was marked by swift leadership changes that disregarded traditional coronation customs. Egypt's growing influence shifted the balance of power, ultimately paving the way for Babylonian dominance. The rapid appointments of new kings during this time reflect the external manipulation of Judah's monarchy and the erosion of its sovereignty.

The cross-references discussed in the previous section reveal a complex methodological framework that links the reigns of monarchs in one kingdom to the rise of their counterparts in a rival kingdom. Scholars generally agree that these cross-references do not consistently align a king's ascension in one realm with the start of a sole reign in the other. Rather, such synchronisms may originate from a coregency, an initial vice-regency, or even a period following abdication.

A notable example is Joram, son of Jehoshaphat. The timeline referenced for his reign aligns with the beginning of Jehoram's sole reign in Israel. This suggests that the point of reference was Joram's prominent vice-regency. While the system of cross-referencing might initially appear erratic, a deeper examination reveals an underlying rationale that correlates with when a king actually began to wield power.

Some monarchs exercised substantial authority from the outset of their coregency, while others remained subordinate until their predecessor's death. In Joram's case, his father Jehoshaphat, although competent, consistently delegated royal authority to his son. This resulted in Joram assuming considerable leadership while his father was still alive. Consequently, the structure of cross-references in the biblical texts appears to follow the actual dynamics of power more than formal enthronement dates.

This leads us to the scholarly work of Edwin Thiele, whose interpretation of 2 Kings 17 and 18 underscores the difficulty of reconciling biblical chronology with Assyrian historical records. Although Thiele aimed to harmonize these accounts, his framework often falters under scrutiny. To sustain his interpretation, he overlooks key chronological markers within the biblical narrative, an approach that compromises both the historical integrity of the text and its theological significance.

Thiele contends that certain chronological inconsistencies in 2 Kings 17 and 18 are the result of later editorial revisions. These, he argues, reordered the original succession of kings. Based on this claim, he constructs a timeline that appears internally coherent and aligned with known Assyrian history. However, such a reconstruction implies intentional manipulation of Israel's chronology to fit his theoretical model, a methodology that falls short of rigorous scholarly standards.

Issues Arising from Thiele's Treatment of 2 Kings 17 and 18

Had Thiele given greater prominence to his analysis of Israel's final monarchs, his thesis might have been received differently. This section of the narrative reveals a compelling case of historical revisionism that challenges the credibility of the timeline he proposes. A careful review of 2 Kings 17 and 18 suggests that these events occurred much closer to the actual composition of the Books of Kings than many earlier accounts. This proximity offers a revealing lens through which to examine the flaws in Thiele's assumptions and invites a broader discussion about the inherent challenges of constructing a cohesive historical chronology from ancient texts.

Synchronisms with Assyrian Historical Events

James Ussher's historical framework is rich with references to the Assyrian Empire. However, his insights into the lineage of Assyrian kings rely heavily on ancient sources such as Eusebius, Sextus Julius Africanus, and others (Ussher, 1650, ref. 578). An examination of Eusebius's writings reveals significant discrepancies between his timelines and the modern understanding of Assyrian history, which is informed by the discovery of the Assyrian Eponym Lists in the nineteenth century. Ussher's portrayals, though earnest, were limited by the resources available to him in the 17th century.

In *The Annals*, Ussher writes:

"When Shalmaneser died, his son Sennacherib reigned in his stead" (APC Tobit 1:18).

"This command the prophet is said to have received in the year when Tartan was sent by Sargon, king of Assyria, who besieged Ashdod and took it."

Sargon is also called Sennacherib (Ussher, 1650, refs. 640-641).

In the 17th century, Bishop Ussher identified Sargon (mentioned once in Isaiah) as another name for Sennacherib, due to the limited historical records available at the time. This reflects the challenges early historians faced in reconstructing ancient timelines based on incomplete information.

These statements underscore the challenges of distinguishing between similarly named rulers and understanding their timelines. Ussher's work reveals the intricate layering of biblical and extrabiblical history, but also the risks of conflation in the absence of archaeological corroboration.

Opinion

While Ussher's framework is both ambitious and foundational in early biblical historiography, it reflects the limitations of pre-modern scholarship. His reliance on secondary sources like Eusebius, who lacked access to modern archaeological data, resulted in genealogies and reigns that often conflict with what we now know from the Assyrian Eponym Lists and other inscriptions.

The discovery of Sargon II's palace complex at Khorsabad in the 1840s marked a turning point in understanding the Assyrian Empire. This architectural marvel not only affirmed Sargon's historical existence but also clarified his relationship with Sennacherib. Contrary to earlier beliefs that merged their identities, evidence now confirms that Sargon and Sennacherib were distinct rulers, father and son, who likely ruled concurrently throughout Sargon's reign — a topic explored in a later chapter.

The Book of Tobit stands as an enigma within the archaeological and historical landscape, profoundly shaping modern interpretations of ancient narratives. James Ussher, the renowned theologian and Bishop of the Church of Ireland, cites this text, considered apocryphal by many Protestant traditions due to its exclusion from the Tanakh and rejection by Jewish authorities. The claim that Tobit was written roughly five centuries after the events it describes raises important questions about its historical reliability. Furthermore, the book's portrayal of Sennacherib as the son of Shalmaneser V reflects a conflation of these figures that demands critical scrutiny.

This narrative invites scholars to reassess the foundations of their historical understanding. It challenges them to critically evaluate the legacies of revered figures and to question widely accepted assumptions. The interaction between Sargon and Sennacherib exemplifies the fluid and evolving nature of historical interpretation.

Thiele and the Assyrian Eponym Lists

Edwin Thiele examined the Assyrian Eponym Lists, first uncovered by Sir Henry Rawlinson in 1846. These lists record each year by naming a high official, an eponym, along with brief descriptions of significant events. By piecing together fragments from multiple copies, scholars have constructed a largely reliable chronological framework for much of the Neo-Assyrian Empire. Assyriologists use this timeline to date events both within Assyria and in neighboring kingdoms that confronted Assyrian power.

A crucial step in establishing this chronology was linking it to a well-dated astronomical event. One eponym list entry reads:

"Bur-Sagale of Guzana, revolt in Assur. In the month of Simanu, a solar eclipse occurred."

Through mathematical study of solar eclipses, this event has been identified as occurring on June 15, 763 BCE. Subsequent events in the following century align well with known historical facts. Yet, dating events before this eclipse remains difficult. Despite these uncertainties, Thiele notably chose to overlook the reservations expressed by Assyriologist Luckenbill about the precision of Assyrian chronology prior to this anchor point.

Debates on the Assyrian Timeline

Since the emergence of Assyriology as a formal discipline, scholars have debated the reliability of Assyrian records. Reverend D. H. Haigh, writing in the *Zeitschrift für Ägyptische Sprache* in August 1871, highlighted a nineteen-year gap in the Assyrian record between 843 and 824 BCE. Haigh questioned Tiglath-Pileser III's claim that Hoshea became king during his reign, suggesting instead that this event belongs to Sargon's time. He also argued that Samaria fell under Assyrian control during Sennacherib's rule.

Haigh was incorrect on both counts. Tiglath-Pileser III conquered much of the Levant, including parts of Israel, and installed Hoshea as a vassal king. Hoshea initially paid tribute but later rebelled, leading to the kingdom's downfall. Though Sargon II claimed credit for capturing Samaria 15 years later, the evidence—supported by the chart—points to Shalmaneser V as the actual conqueror.

Other authorities, such as Canon Rawlinson and Ernest de Bunsen, argued that Pul ruled just before Tiglath-Pileser, underscoring the complexities and disagreements surrounding Assyrian history. However, modern scholarship has confirmed that Pul and Tiglath-Pileser were, in fact, the same person.

The Nineteen-Year Gap and Queen Shammu-ramat

To understand this nineteen-year gap, Haigh linked it to the turbulent period following the death of Shalmaneser III and preceding the reign of Shamsi-Adad V. This era saw civil strife as heirs contended violently for the throne. Haigh's theory offers valuable insight into discrepancies between Assyrian and biblical chronologies, prompting a reevaluation of this critical juncture.

Haigh calculated the gap as nineteen years; however, based on my own calculations — as illustrated in the chart and supported by the subsequent discussion of

Shammuramat's reign — the period extends to twenty-one years, from 830/29 to 810/09 BCE. This adjustment profoundly affects our understanding of the ancient Near East and compels us to revisit the historical narrative.

Central to this revised timeline is Queen Shammu-ramat, a figure often overlooked in mainstream histories. Known as the Warrior Queen of Assyria, she served as Queen Regent for twenty-one years after her husband, Shamsi-Adad V, died when their son was still a child. Even after Adad-Nirari III ascended the throne, Shammu-ramat likely maintained substantial influence, effectively sharing royal authority until her death.

Looking Ahead

Building on Haigh's insights requires careful accumulation of evidence, a task we will pursue in the following chapters. These discussions will illuminate the intricate ties between the Assyrian and Hebrew monarchies and underscore the pivotal role played by Shammu-ramat.

As we explore the complexities of Middle Eastern history, we will recognize the remarkable individuals who shaped it, most notably, a powerful female leader whose legacy challenges traditional narratives of ancient power.

The previous paragraph aims to clarify the difficulties in reconciling two distinct timelines, rather than to confuse those seeking straightforward answers. Thiele, unaware of the twenty-one-year gap in his calculations, was nonetheless forced to attempt compressing the timeline by those 21 years, which often led to convoluted interpretations. This confusion is further compounded by Tiglath-Pileser III's apparent attempts to distort historical records, obscuring the timeline's clarity.

To resolve this chronological puzzle, we must adopt assumptions that differ from Thiele's framework. This alternative approach allows us to reconcile the Biblical narrative while simultaneously questioning the reliability of some Assyrian records.

Our objective is to construct an Absolute Chronology of the Divided Kingdom, employing mathematical methods and pattern recognition to bridge the early synchronisms found in both historical accounts.

A key element in Thiele's argument involves references to Ahab on the Kurkh Stele and Jehu on the Black Obelisk, both associated with the reign of Shalmaneser III. However, as we will examine in due course, Thiele's conclusions regarding these synchronisms are flawed.

CHAPTER 3

The first chapter proposed that the rival kingdoms of Israel and Judah employed a specific system to track their histories. If this idea proves incorrect, it could complicate efforts to understand their timelines. Many historians, such as Ussher and Thiele, primarily rely on a different method, which has heavily influenced biblical chronology studies. This reliance fosters the impression that grasping the biblical account requires navigating complex and often convoluted approaches. Historically, scholars have exercised caution, tentatively accepting provisional theories until more robust alternatives emerge. Consequently, it is crucial to clarify the origins of the information.

Who Authored the Books of Kings and Chronicles?

Scribes faithfully compiled the Books of Kings and Chronicles from numerous historical sources.

Scholars generally agree that the Books of Kings were compiled around 560–540 BCE, though the precise identities of the authors remain unknown. Tradition suggests that the prophets Jeremiah and/or Ezekiel may have contributed to the original compilation, then a single volume. However, the final section, which records Jehoiachin's release from captivity, was added after both prophets had died.

Thus, while these figures may have played significant roles, unnamed scribes ultimately completed the work. This situation mirrors the final verses of Deuteronomy, which describe Moses's death.

These scribes demonstrated deep historical knowledge and the skill to craft a coherent narrative by weaving together over four centuries of material. The texts themselves reveal that they drew on several now-lost sources, including:

- The Book of the Acts of Solomon (1 Kings 11:41)

- The Chronicles of the Kings of Judah (1 Kings 14:29)

- The Chronicles of the Kings of Israel (1 Kings 14:19; 16:14; 16:20; 2 Kings 1:18; 14:28; 15:21)

- The Book of Shemaiah and of Iddo the Seer (2 Chronicles 9:29; 12:15; 13:22), also known as The Story of the Prophet Iddo or The Annals of the Prophet Iddo

- The Annals of King David (1 Chronicles 27:24), also called The Chronicles of King David

- The Book of Gad the Seer (1 Chron. 29:29)

- The Prophecy of Ahijah (2 Chron. 9:29)

- The Book of Nathan the Prophet (1 Chronicles 29:29; 2 Chronicles 9:29)

- The Book of Jehu (2 Chronicles 20:34)

- The Vision of Isaiah (2 Chron. 32:32)

- The Acts of Uzziah (2 Chronicles 26:22), possibly identical to the Book of Isaiah

- The Acts of the Kings of Israel (2 Chronicles 33:18), possibly the same as The Book of the Kings of Israel

- The Sayings of the Seers (2 Chronicles 33:19)

The Books of Kings and Chronicles draw from this diverse corpus to construct their historical narratives. Understanding the context of the Judean captivity in Babylon is essential to grasping the scribes' intentions. These editors crafted a nuanced retelling of the Kings, emphasizing cultural identity and religious fidelity. Their goal was to guide the Hebrew people, encouraging them to honor the "true God," as Jeremiah 10:10 emphasizes.

The Books of Chronicles are believed to have been compiled around 460 BCE. The authors used a source referred to as "The Story of the Book of Kings" (2 Chronicles 24:27), which connects directly to the Books of Kings. Scholarly debate continues over the authorship of Ezra and Nehemiah and the possibility that Ezra himself compiled Chronicles.

Closing the Historical Loop

The Books of Kings conclude with Jehoiachin's release from captivity after thirty-seven years, while Chronicles dates slightly later. Genealogical records in 1 Chronicles 3:17–24 trace Jehoiachin's descendants through six generations, implying approximately 120 years passed since his captivity at age eighteen, with a margin of about twenty years.

Around the time of Cyrus's decree permitting Jews to return to Jerusalem, the Samaritans opposed the returnees. Led by Zerubbabel, Jehoiachin's grandson, and High Priest Joshua, many Jews returned around 520–515 BCE to rebuild the Second Temple. However, by the mid-400s BCE, during Ezra and Nehemiah's time, Jerusalem remained in a state of disrepair. Social issues abounded: wealthy Jews exploited the poor through slavery and usury, as detailed in Nehemiah 5. Additionally, many Jews had ceased using the Hebrew language, threatening cultural continuity. Nehemiah's reforms sought to address these concerns.

Different Purposes, Complementary Narratives

The Book of Kings aimed primarily to inspire exiled Jews to worship Yahweh, linking divine favor to faithful worship. In contrast, Chronicles served a different purpose. Its genealogical records helped returning exiles reclaim their identities, especially eleven of the twelve tribes, excluding Dan due to its idolatry. Chronicles also highlights the achievements of Kings David and Solomon, offering a narrative that resonated with the returning diaspora. It provides valuable chronological details that aid modern study of this formative period in Jewish history.

The Argument for Accession Accounting: An Academic Analysis

The concept of accession accounting in ancient historical records is a fascinating subject. The scribes who compiled these documents had access to archives from both Israel and Judah, including many texts referenced in Scripture. Each kingdom likely kept detailed records of the other's events, especially concerning kings and their successions.

The phrase "history is written by the victors" rings particularly true here. After the Assyrian Empire absorbed Israel (Samaria), the Judeans inherited the responsibility of preserving the historical narrative. Yet during their seventy-year exile in Babylon, they faced the gradual erosion of their cultural and religious identity.

It is probable that Judean scribes had access to records containing detailed accounts of the Israelite monarchy's kings. Considering Thiele's theory that Israel may have used a different accounting method, similar to that of the Assyrians, it raises the question: did the Judean scribes attempt to reconcile or correct inconsistencies in the Israelite records?

It seems unlikely that scribes with access to both sets of records would overlook chronological discrepancies. More plausibly, they synthesized the information into a unified system that reflected history through a Judean lens.

Scholars often point to a bias in the Hebrew Scriptures, especially in the predominantly negative portrayal of Israelite kings. This observation prompts a critical question: could this bias have influenced how chronological data was recorded? If so, it is doubtful that more nuanced details, such as non-accession accounting, would have been preserved in the biblical texts.

Textual Sources of the Old Testament

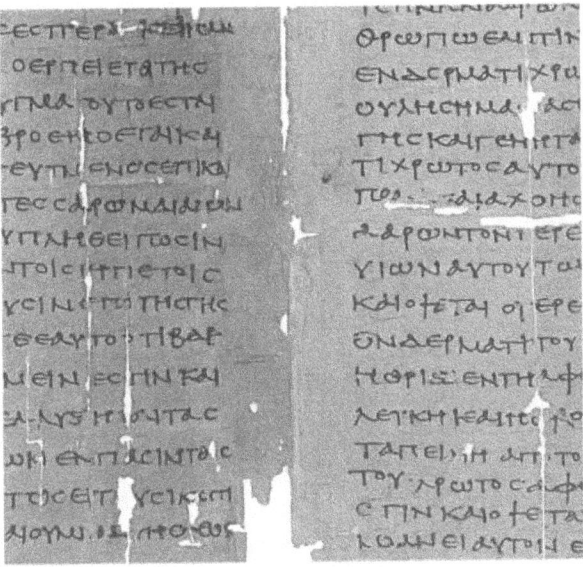

The Greek texts were widely used in the Early Church as Greek was the dominant language of the region.

While the Old Testament has expanded beyond the the five books of the Law, its core messages and historical narratives have remained intact. The scribes' access to diverse records enabled them to integrate various sources for a fuller understanding. Many Christians refer to the Bible as "The Living Word," and the Old Testament itself has functioned as a living document, growing in size and scope until the completion of the Book of Malachi.

It is particularly interesting to consider which Old Testament versions Jesus, His disciples, and the Apostle Paul used. Over ninety percent of the more than three hundred scriptural references made by Jesus and His followers derive from the Septuagint, with some from Hebrew texts and Aramaic Targums. Similarly, Paul quoted Old Testament scriptures one hundred and eighty-three times, showing a strong preference for the Septuagint.

The Masoretic Text, finalized in the tenth century CE, closely resembles the Septuagint, with mostly minor differences. Both versions have informed this study.

Perspectives on the Septuagint and Masoretic Text

Many modern scholars are skeptical of the Septuagint, and most contemporary Bible translations primarily rely on the Jewish Masoretic Text (MT), compiled between the seventh and tenth centuries CE. Exploring the differences between these texts is vital, especially within their theological and historical contexts.

Before dismissing the Septuagint in favor of the MT tradition, it is important to recognize the Septuagint's value to the Early Church. After Alexander the Great defeated Darius III of Persia, Judah became a vassal state within the Hellenistic empire. Following Alexander's death, his empire fragmented; Judah first came under Antigonus I's rule, then the Seleucid dynasty from 301 BCE until the Roman takeover.

Greek emerged as the lingua franca of the Middle East during this period. Around 270 BCE, the Septuagint, a Greek translation of the Hebrew Scriptures, was produced in Alexandria and circulated among Greek-speaking Jews.

Antiochus IV Epiphanes, who ruled from 175 to 163 BCE, was notorious for his hostility toward Jewish traditions. His epithet "Epiphanes" (meaning "divine") was bitterly mocked as "Epimanes" ("the madman") due to his oppressive reign. He enforced Hellenistic customs on the Jews, triggering the Maccabean Revolt. His regime destroyed Hebrew Scriptures and imposed death penalties on those who preserved them.

Sources and Approach for This Study

The sources used in the forthcoming analysis primarily come from the King James Version of the Bible, supplemented by references to the Septuagint when noted. If textual differences have affected the precision of chronological data, reaching a definitive conclusion may prove difficult. Thiele strongly advocates the reliability of the Hebrew chronology, asserting that "...Professor Thiele demonstrates conclusively that, in reality, these Hebrew chronological numbers were transmitted 'without often becoming corrupt'" (Thiele, 1986, p. 30).

The following chapters will carefully examine his argument in depth.

Analysing the Metrics of Monarchic Tenures:

When studying historical reigns, early Christian-era researchers could have conducted more thorough analyses had they fully grasped the complexities of the documentation. However, details about vice regencies and coregencies are often unclear or incomplete, requiring a trial-and-error approach, much like the method Thiele employed to reach his conclusions (Thiele, 1983, p. 29). Deduction remains a powerful tool in interpreting historical evidence.

Many analytical problems boil down to simple algebraic forms: $\mathbf{a} = \mathbf{b} + \mathbf{c}$, where $\mathbf{b}$ and $\mathbf{c}$ are known. High school students can solve such problems easily, though some are more challenging. Aside from a few exceptions, these calculations rarely demand excessive intellectual effort.

Yet, it is crucial to consider the unique circumstances surrounding each reign. Although accession principles remain consistent, variations may confuse those less comfortable with numbers. To aid understanding, the results will be presented in a structured five-page chart.

Key Dates for the Divided Kingdoms

- **Nisan 952 BCE:** Start of Jeroboam I's reign in Israel

- **Tishri 952 BCE:** Beginning of Rehoboam's rule in Judah

We will analyze reigns chronologically and explain the calculations behind these dates. The charts will demonstrate how the numerical data align with the durations stated in Scripture.

It is important to remember that when a historical source notes that a monarch in Kingdom A began his reign during the seventeenth year of King B's rule, one must consider the different new year start dates for each kingdom. These calendar differences can create apparent timeline discrepancies; for example, the period described as the seventeenth year might more accurately be interpreted as sixteen and a half years, not seventeen.

Explanation of the Charts

The charts cater to visual learners by representing the timeline graphically. Lengths of reigns appear in varying shades to highlight intervals and overlaps. Without these visual aids, this project would have been far more difficult to undertake.

Cross-references are marked with black lines and arrows, indicating where each reference begins and ends. Years are based on the Julian calendar and broken down by quarters, with the second and fourth quarters aligning with the Jewish months of Nisan and Tishri.

Each chart conveys detailed information with nuance. Reign durations and their corresponding scriptural citations are well documented. Year numbers often carry a suffix, 't' for Tishri (September/October) and 'n' for Nisan (March/April), to indicate the calendar reference.

Core Assumption: Anchoring the Timeline

The timeline of the Divided Kingdom centers on the reign of Jehoiachin, historically recorded from **December 9, 598 BCE** to **March 15 or 16, 597 BCE**. The Nebuchadnezzar Chronicle states Jehoiachin's reign ended on the second day of Adar during Nebuchadnezzar's seventh year, aligning with those March dates. This timing reflects the Babylonian calendar's sunset-to-sunset day cycle.

Scholar Leo Depuydt emphasizes that while Ptolemy's Canon is astronomically accurate, it does not guarantee historical precision. Ptolemy traced dates back to Nabonassar's reign, beginning in 626/625 BCE, raising concerns about the reliability of mixing astronomical data with historical narratives.

A lunar eclipse dated April 22, 620 BCE (Julian), noted by Ptolemy, is pivotal in Babylonian chronology, marking Nabonassar's fifth year. Traditionally, this date has gone unquestioned. However, recent research by Faulstich challenges this, pointing out that Ptolemy assigned thirteen years to Assaradinus (Esarhaddon), while Babylonian Chronicles record only twelve. Faulstich proposes shifting the eclipse to Nabonassar's sixth year, which in turn adjusts Jehoiachin's capture date to 2 Adar 598 BCE, effectively moving the timeline one year earlier.

Refining the Reference Point for Jehoiachin (Jeconiah)

Scholarly debate around Faulstich's work suggests revising Jehoiachin's capture date by one year earlier. However, this analysis argues for an additional one-year adjustment to achieve precise chronological alignment.

Just before Jehoiachin's reign, his predecessors, Jehoahaz and Jehoiakim, contributed one extra year that is traditionally unaccounted for in the timeline. Jehoahaz became king in Tishri 611, but this appointment insulted Pharaoh Necho II, who was returning from the Battle of Harran. Necho II subsequently imprisoned Jehoahaz, yet officials still counted his reign as three months, even during his imprisonment.

Necho II appointed Jehoiakim in the fourth month. He reigned for the nine month

49

balance of 611, which is counted as his Zero Year. The official beginning of his eleven-year reign started in Tishri 610. This decision effectively added a year to the timeline.

As a result, the revised reference date for Jehoiachin's capture is 2 Adar, 598 BCE. For any calculations before 610, the extra year has pushed the timeline back by another year.

Additional Historical Note

Once the fully reconciled chart of the Divided Kingdom was complete, it used the traditional date for Jehoiachin's capture as the reference point. However, it quickly became apparent that there was an issue: the calculations indicate that the date for the defeat of Samaria was 720 BCE. While researchers consider dates before 800 BCE questionable, they have well established the date of the defeat of Samaria at 722 BCE. This specific historical date prompted the investigation into why the date for 597 BCE was incorrect.

Final Note

The charts clearly illustrate the reigns of Israel's kings during the Divided Kingdom. Bookmarking or copying these pages will help readers navigate the more complex calculations with greater ease. Researchers can purchase a high-resolution integrated chart from the author's website, which can be printed in A2 size for detailed study.

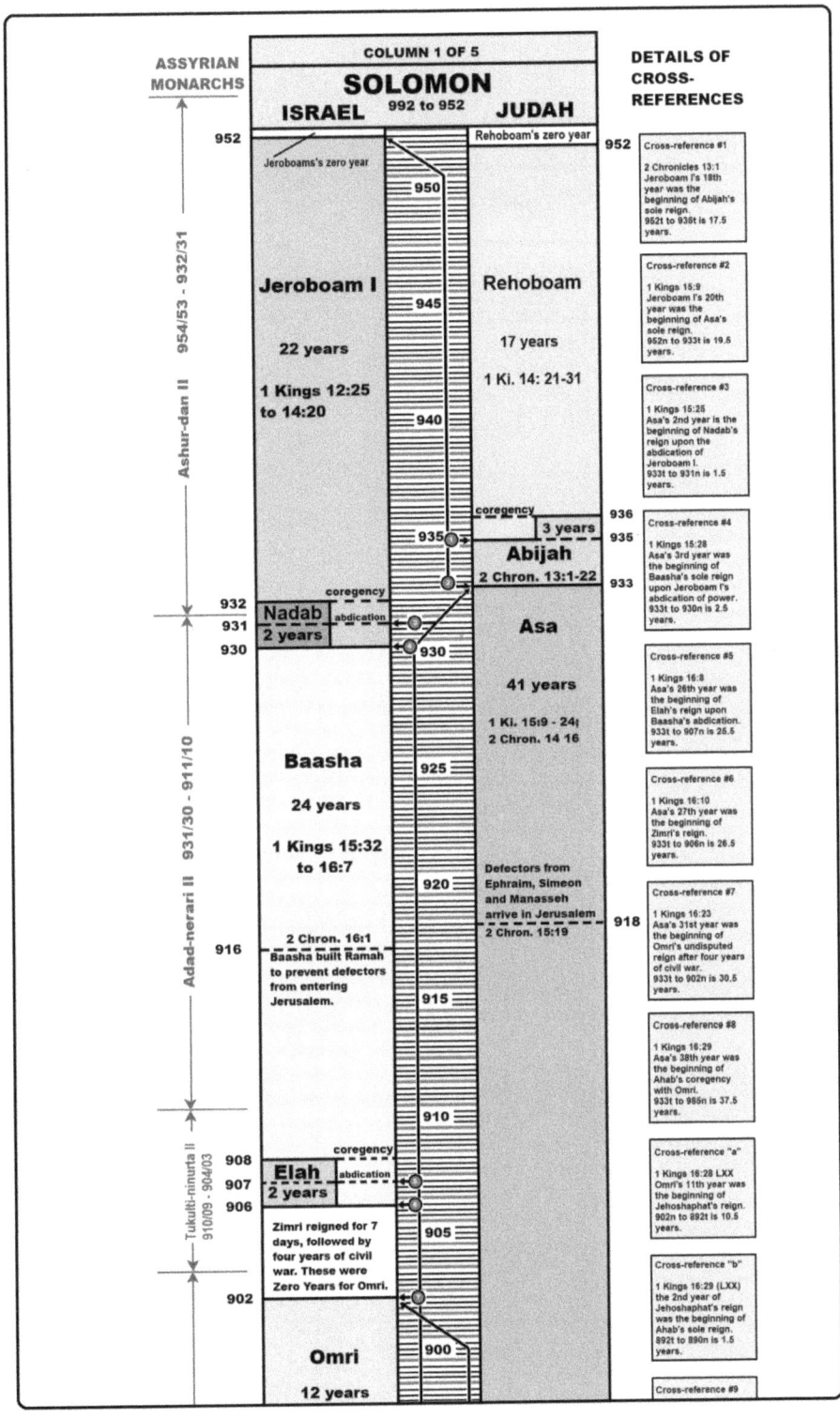

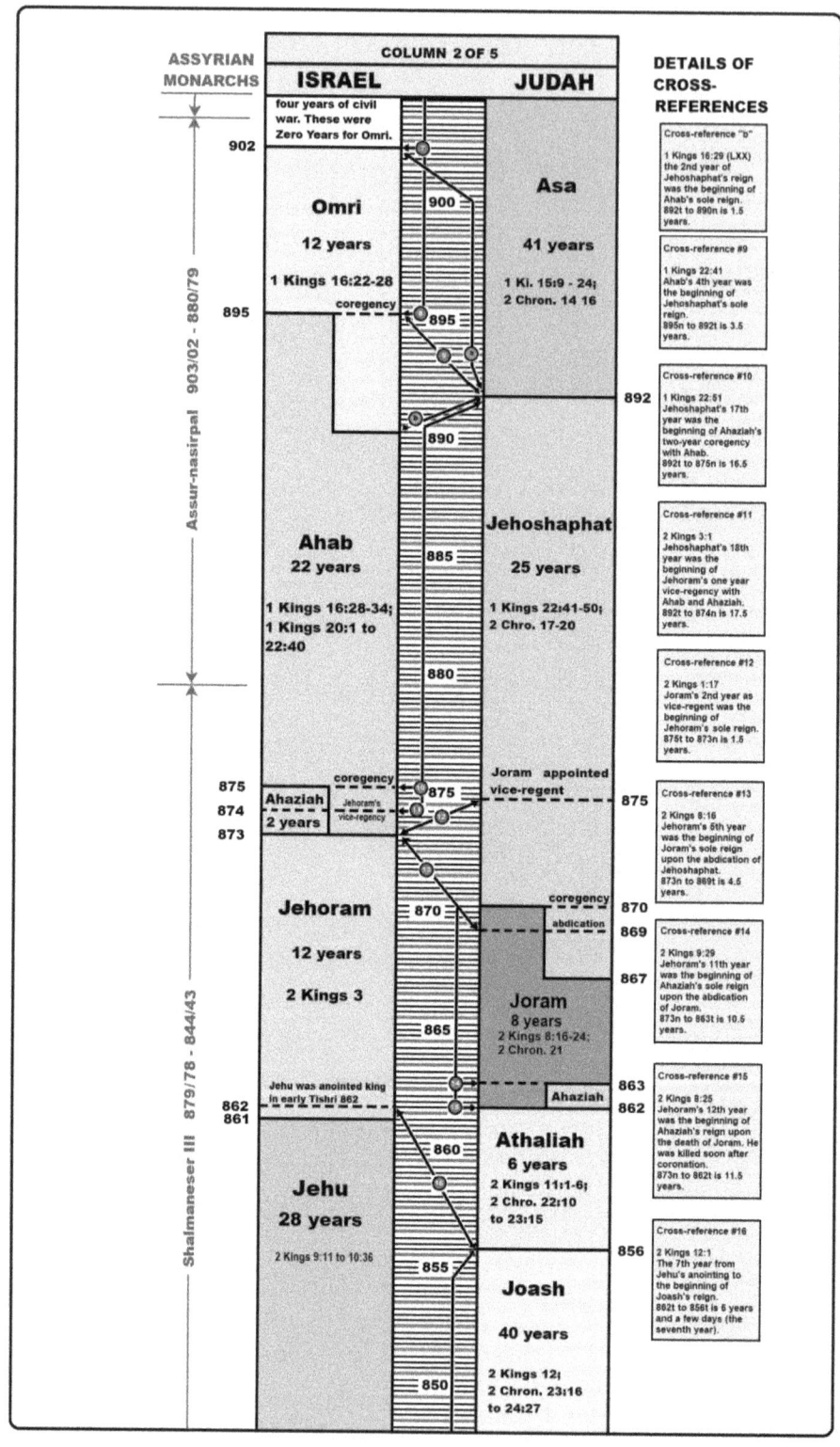

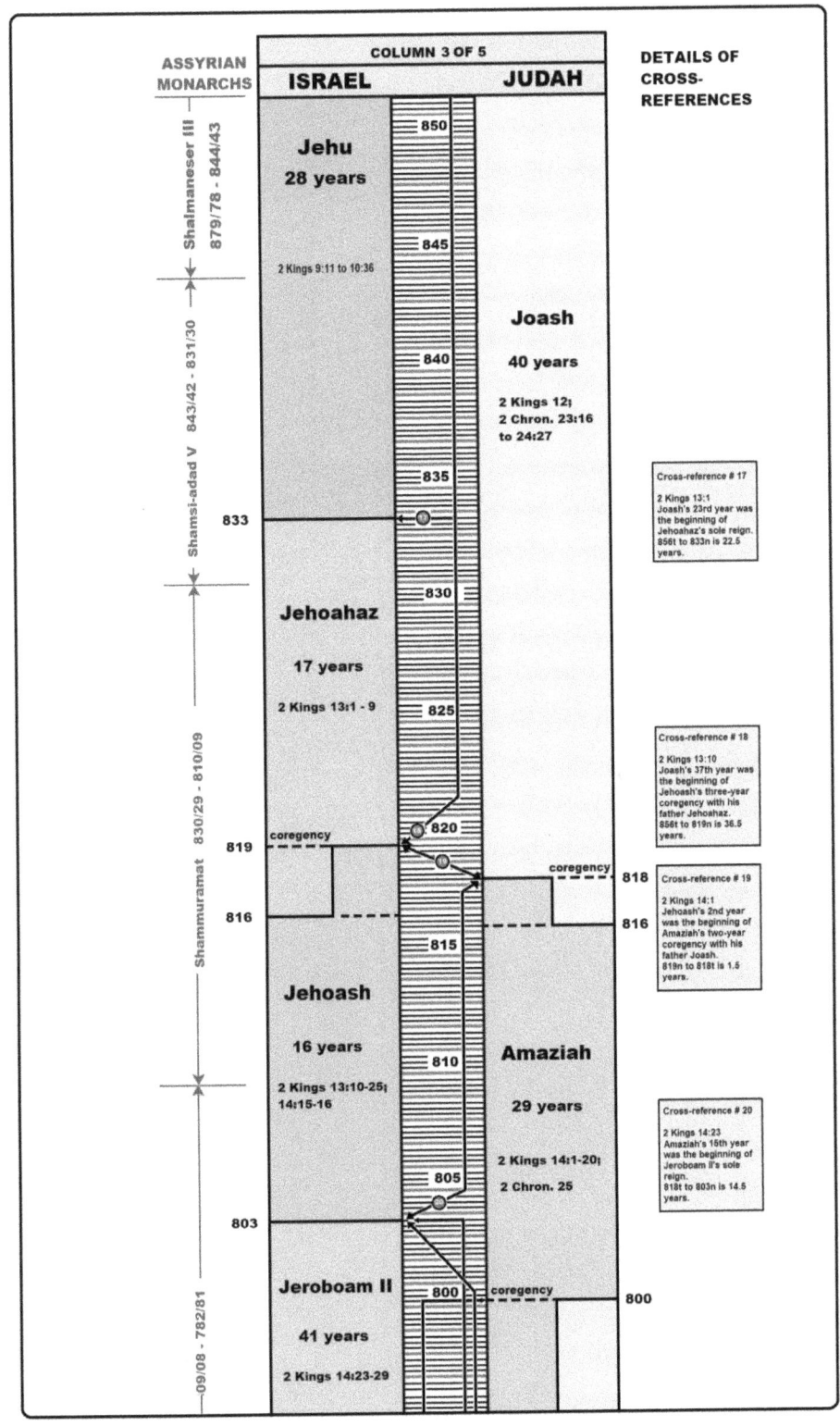

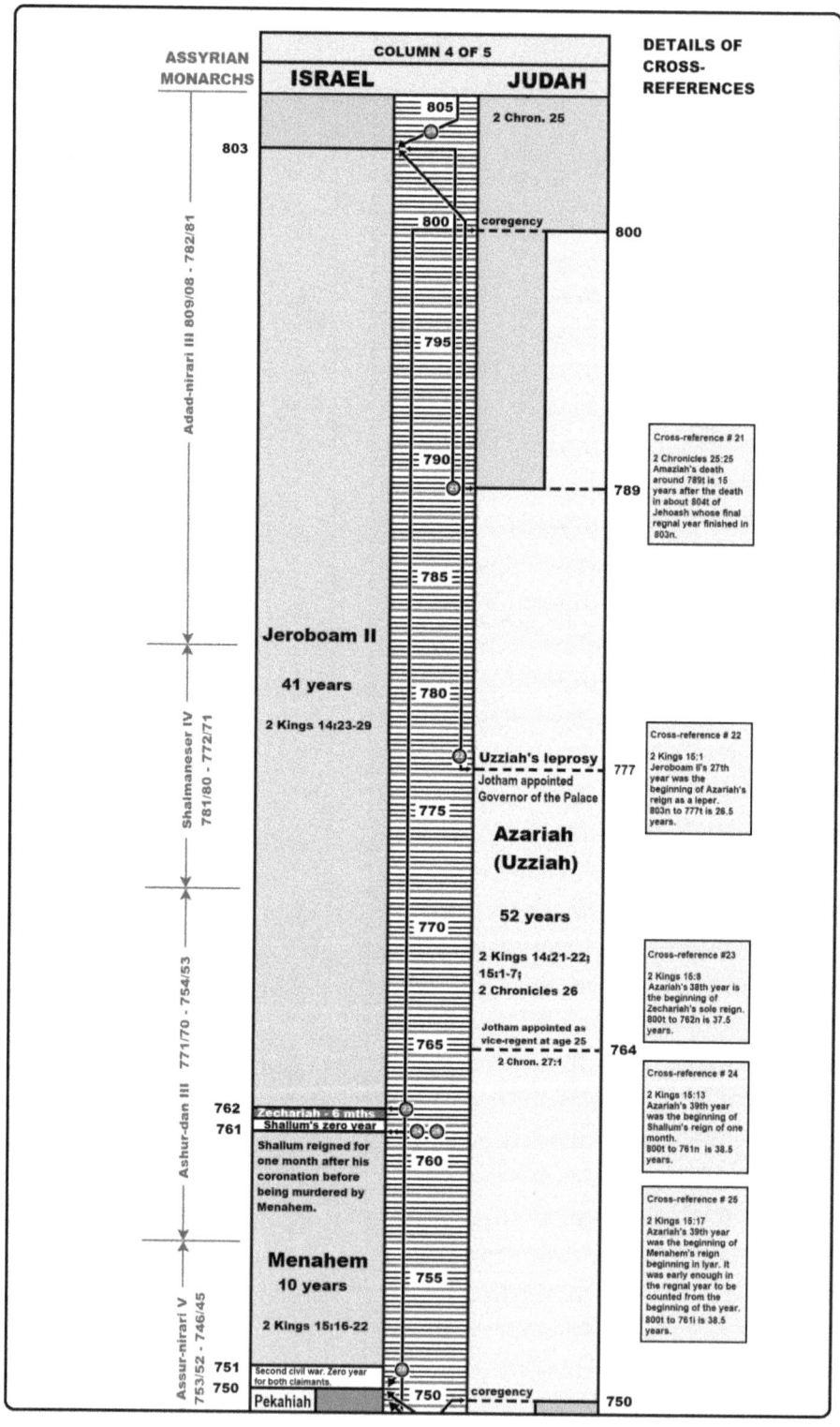

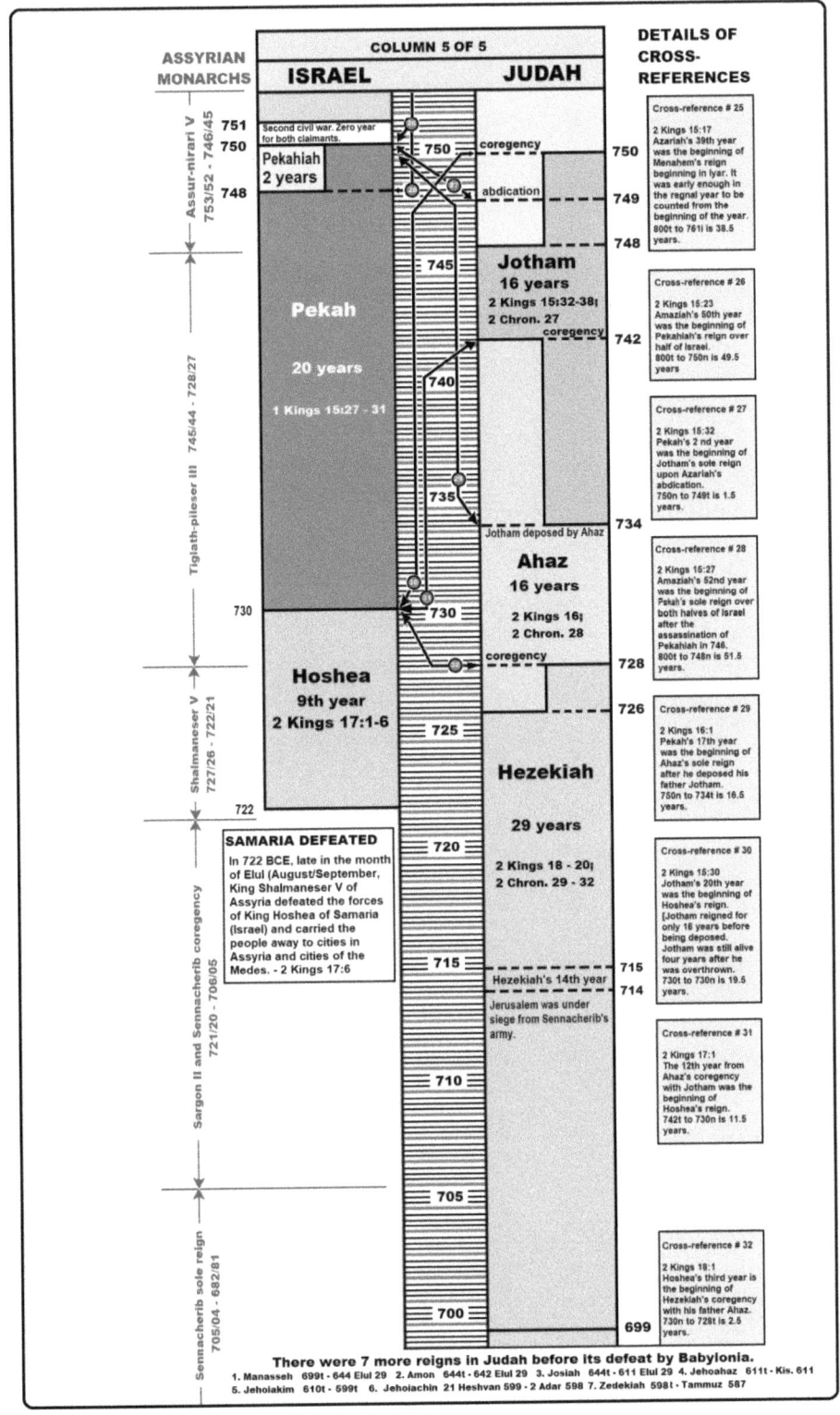

COLUMN 5 OF 5

ASSYRIAN MONARCHS

ISRAEL

JUDAH

DETAILS OF CROSS-REFERENCES

Assur-nirari V 753/52 - 746/45

751 — Second civil war. Zero year for both claimants.

750 — Pekahiah 2 years

750 coregency

748 — abdication

749

748

745

Cross-reference # 25
2 Kings 15:17 Azariah's 39th year was the beginning of Menahem's reign beginning in Iyar. It was early enough in the regnal year to be counted from the beginning of the year. 800t to 761i is 38.5 years.

Jotham 16 years
2 Kings 15:32-38;
2 Chron. 27

coregency 742

Cross-reference # 26
2 Kings 15:23 Amaziah's 50th year was the beginning of Pekahiah's reign over half of Israel. 800t to 750n is 49.5 years

Pekah 20 years
1 Kings 15:27 - 31

Tiglath-pileser III 745/44 - 728/27

740

Cross-reference # 27
2 Kings 15:32 Pekah's 2 nd year was the beginning of Jotham's sole reign upon Azariah's abdication. 750n to 749t is 1.5 years.

735

Jotham deposed by Ahaz 734

Ahaz 16 years
2 Kings 16;
2 Chron. 28

730 — 730

coregency 728

Cross-reference # 28
2 Kings 15:27 Amaziah's 52nd year was the beginning of Pekah's sole reign over both halves of Israel after the assassination of Pekahiah in 746. 800t to 748n is 51.5 years.

726

Hoshea 9th year
2 Kings 17:1-6

725

Hezekiah 29 years
2 Kings 18 - 20;
2 Chron. 29 - 32

Cross-reference # 29
2 Kings 16:1 Pekah's 17th year was the beginning of Ahaz's sole reign after he deposed his father Jotham. 750n to 734t is 16.5 years.

Shalmaneser V 727/26 - 722/21

730

722

722 — **SAMARIA DEFEATED**
In 722 BCE, late in the month of Elul (August/September, King Shalmaneser V of Assyria defeated the forces of King Hoshea of Samaria (Israel) and carried the people away to cities in Assyria and cities of the Medes. - 2 Kings 17:6

720

Cross-reference # 30
2 Kings 15:30 Jotham's 20th year was the beginning of Hoshea's reign. [Jotham reigned for only 16 years before being deposed. Jotham was still alive four years after he was overthrown. 730t to 730n is 19.5 years.]

Sargon II and Sennacherib coregency 721/20 - 706/05

715

715

714

Hezekiah's 14th year
Jerusalem was under siege from Sennacherib's army.

Cross-reference # 31
2 Kings 17:1 The 12th year from Ahaz's coregency with Jotham was the beginning of Hoshea's reign. 742t to 730n is 11.5 years.

710

705

Sennacherib sole reign 705/04 - 682/81

700

699

Cross-reference # 32
2 Kings 18:1 Hoshea's third year is the beginning of Hezekiah's coregency with his father Ahaz. 730n to 728t is 2.5 years.

There were 7 more reigns in Judah before its defeat by Babylonia.
1. Manasseh 699t - 644 Elul 29   2. Amon 644t - 642 Elul 29   3. Josiah 644t - 611 Elul 29   4. Jehoahaz 611t - Kis. 611
5. Jehoiakim 610t - 599t   6. Jehoiachin 21 Heshvan 599 - 2 Adar 598   7. Zedekiah 598t - Tammuz 587

John Ferris

CHAPTER 4

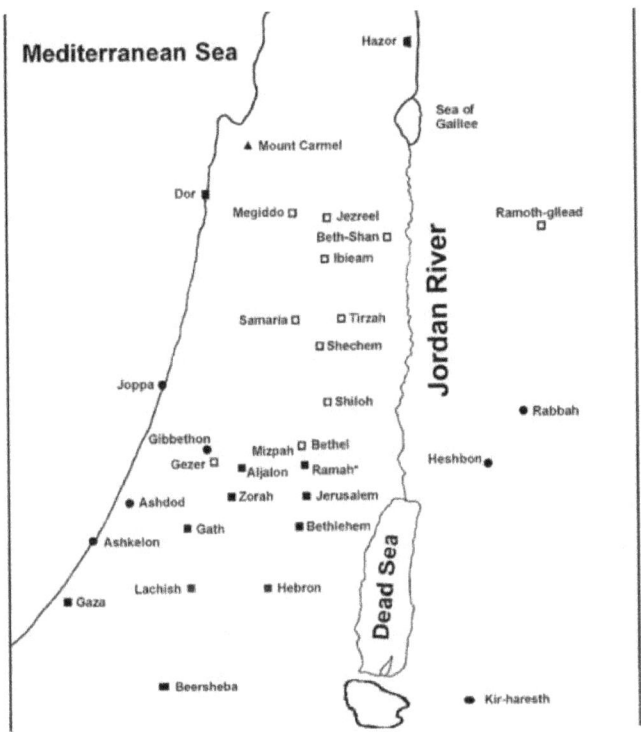

Major cities during the Divided Kingdoms

The Division of the Kingdom of Israel: Historical Context and Dynamics

King Solomon died in late 953 or early 952 BCE. He maintained his authority until the end of his final regnal year, culminating in Nisan of 952 BCE. Solomon's son, Rehoboam, assumed effective control immediately following his father's death. However, his formal coronation did not occur until Tishri 952, resulting in a protracted period often regarded as his "Zero Year." At Solomon's death, the Israelite kingdom remained united.

In a significant turn of events, Jeroboam—formerly a trusted official under Solomon and prophesied by Ahijah to govern over ten of the twelve tribes—had fled to Egypt to escape possible reprisals. Upon hearing of Solomon's death,

Jeroboam returned, reclaiming influence among the northern tribes. He approached Rehoboam with a request:

"Reduce the heavy taxation on the people."

But Rehoboam scornfully refused. This rejection precipitated a pivotal moment in Israel's history. The ten northern tribes broke away, proclaiming Jeroboam king over what became known as the Kingdom of Israel. The remaining two tribes remained loyal to Rehoboam, forming the Kingdom of Judah (1 Kings 11–12). Because of this division, Rehoboam's coronation was postponed and rescheduled for Jerusalem six months later, in Tishri.

The timeline surrounding Solomon's death and Jeroboam's actions is fascinating. The period from the news of Solomon's passing to Jeroboam's return from Egypt and confrontation with Rehoboam would have taken several weeks. Jeroboam likely arrived just before Rehoboam's initially planned coronation in Nisan (March/April). Jeroboam himself was crowned during that same month.

Historically, in the United Kingdom of Israel, coronations took place in Nisan, while Judah's "New Year of Kings" began in Tishri. This tradition dates back to King David, who ruled Judah for seven and a half years before becoming king of all Israel. David's coronation over Israel occurred in Nisan, following his initial Tishri coronation over Judah.

Jeroboam's choice to hold his coronation in Nisan mirrored David's precedent, emphasizing the importance of traditional timing in royal legitimacy. When the rebellion against Rehoboam caused the cancellation of his coronation in Israel, his own coronation in Judah was deferred by six months, aligning with David's practice.

Scholars Franz Xavier Kugler and Valerius Coucke noted this six-month offset, which helps clarify the timeline. Because the northern tribes supported Jeroboam,

Rehoboam had to choose a different date for his coronation—Tishri. This understanding resolves previous difficulties in establishing a clear sequence of events.

Calculating Solomon's Reign (992n to 952 Adar)

Constructing the chronology for the Divided Kingdom required overlaying the Hebrew calendar on the Julian calendar to represent both the Israelite and Judean New Years. The Hebrew months of Nisan and Tishri approximately correspond to March/April and September/October in the Western calendar. Nearly all cross-references on the final timeline begin or end with Nisan and Tishri.

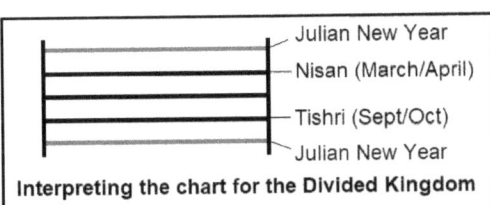

Interpreting the chart for the Divided Kingdom

When completed, the chart was as much a revelation to the author as it will be to new readers. The final pattern fit together seamlessly, showing a zero margin of error—a rare achievement in ancient history, where dates often shift with new discoveries.

Upon Solomon's death in the latter half of his fortieth year, turmoil ensued over high taxation. The narrative picks up in early 952 BCE with Rehoboam's confrontation with a delegation of tribal representatives—including Jeroboam, son of Nebat.

The Reigns of Israel and Judah in Chronological Order

Jeroboam I of Israel (952n to 930 Adar)
Ussher's Dates: 975 to 954 BCE
Thiele's Dates: 931 to 910 BCE

Jeroboam was the son of Nebat, an Ephraimite. Solomon recognized his administrative talents and appointed him supervisor of public works around Jerusalem. During this service, Jeroboam grew discontent with Solomon's excesses and plotted to become king. When Solomon discovered this, Jeroboam fled to Egypt, seeking refuge with Pharaoh Shishak—believed to be Shoshenq I of Egypt's Twenty-second Dynasty.

When news of Solomon's death reached Egypt in late 953 or early 952 BCE, Jeroboam swiftly returned. He joined a delegation petitioning Rehoboam to ease Solomon's heavy taxes. When Rehoboam refused, the ten northern tribes withdrew allegiance from David's house and proclaimed Jeroboam king. Rehoboam was forced to abandon his planned coronation in Nisan 952 BCE at Shechem.

Instead, Jeroboam was crowned king of the newly formed Northern Kingdom of Israel in Nisan at Shechem. Meanwhile, Rehoboam fled to Jerusalem and became king over Judah, comprising the tribes of Judah and Benjamin. Because Rehoboam's coronation in Nisan was canceled, and due to accession rules, his coronation was postponed until Tishri—the seventh month—which coincided with the New Year for neighboring nations.

Consequently, the two kingdoms were forever separated by six months in their regnal year reckoning: Israel began its regnal years in Nisan, while Judah began in Tishri, six months later.

During Jeroboam's reign, military conflicts with Judah continued along their contested border. A major concern for Jeroboam was the Hebrew Scriptures' requirement that Jerusalem serve as the central place of worship. Specifically, the Torah mandated three annual pilgrimages—collectively called the *Shalosh Regalim*: Pesach (Passover), Shavuot (Weeks), and Sukkot (Booths). Every Hebrew male was expected to participate in these pilgrimages each year.

To prevent his subjects from traveling to worship in enemy territory, Jeroboam instituted what became known as "the sins of Jeroboam." He established a rival religious system by setting up golden calves in Dan to the north and Bethel to the south (1 Kings 12:28–30). Additionally, he stationed sentinels along the border with Judah to block pilgrim access.

Jeroboam also introduced a competing festival. As recorded in 1 Kings 12:32 (NLT):

"And Jeroboam instituted a religious festival in Bethel, held on the fifteenth day of the eighth month, in imitation of the annual Festival of Shelters (Booths) in Judah. There at Bethel, he himself offered sacrifices to the calves he had made, and he appointed priests for the pagan shrines he had established."

To further consolidate his break from traditional worship, Jeroboam likely authorized alterations to the Scriptures to support his religious reforms. The Samaritan Pentateuch, which survives today, differs from the Jewish Pentateuch in about 6,000 places—many minor but some significant. Notably, the Samaritan text emphasizes Mount Gerizim (near Shechem) as the divinely chosen site for worship and sacrifice, contrasting with the Jerusalem-centered worship of Judah.

Later kings of Israel who followed Jeroboam's religious practices are described as "walking in the way of Jeroboam." Interestingly, the phrase "the sins of Jeroboam" appears seventeen times exclusively in the Books of Kings; it is absent from the Books of Chronicles.

In the later years of Jeroboam's reign, Abijah of Judah came to power with the goal of reuniting the two kingdoms by defeating Jeroboam. Abijah scored a decisive victory, killing 500,000 of Israel's 800,000-strong army. After Abijah's death— after only three years on the throne—Israel was left significantly weakened, diminishing Jeroboam's ability to threaten Judah.

Jeroboam appointed his son Nadab as coregent two years before his death. One year later, Jeroboam abdicated, and Nadab became sole king—only to be assassinated at Gibbethon within that same year.

Rehoboam of Judah (952t – 935 Elul)

For reference: Ussher's dates – 975 to 958 BCE; Thiele's dates – 931 to 913 BCE

King Solomon was renowned for wisdom and wealth, receiving tribute from many nations. However, despite a strong start, his final years were marked by excess: Solomon had 700 wives and 300 concubines, mostly princesses (1 Kings 11:3). Many marriages were politically motivated to secure peace, but they led Solomon to idolatry, building temples for foreign gods.

According to 1 Kings 11:9–13 (NLT):

"The Lord was very angry with Solomon because his heart had turned away from the Lord, the God of Israel, who had appeared to him twice. The Lord had specifically warned Solomon about worshipping other gods, but Solomon did not listen to the Lord's command.

Therefore, the Lord said to him, 'Since you have not kept my covenant and have disobeyed my decrees, I will surely tear the kingdom away from you and give it to one of your servants. However, for the sake of your father, David, I will not do this while you are still alive. I will take the kingdom away from your son, but I will not take away the entire kingdom; I will let him be king of one tribe, for the sake of my servant David and for the sake of Jerusalem, my chosen city.'"

When Rehoboam inherited the throne, he also inherited his father's arrogance and excess. He had 18 wives and 60 concubines, who bore him 28 sons and 60 daughters (2 Chronicles 11:21). When tribal elders pleaded for tax relief, Rehoboam refused. Consequently, the ten northern tribes abandoned his kingship.

They rejected his planned coronation and instead crowned Jeroboam king. Rehoboam fled to Judah and was crowned king of Judah in Tishri. This mirrored King David's initial coronation over Judah following Saul's death. Saul's son Ishbosheth ruled the northern tribes for two years before being assassinated, after which David reunited the kingdom, reigning forty years.

2 Chronicles 12:2 states:

"King Shishak of Egypt came up and attacked Jerusalem in the fifth year of King Rehoboam's reign."

Updated chronology places this event in 948/47 BCE. After the attack, Judah became a vassal state of Egypt, confirmed by inscriptions at Karnak's Bubasite Portal.

Rehoboam and Jeroboam remained at war throughout their reigns (2 Chronicles 12:15). Near the end of Rehoboam's rule, he appointed his son Abijah as coregent. While not explicitly documented, the coregency is inferred from the following verses:

- 2 Chronicles 13:1: "Abijah began to rule over Judah in the eighteenth year of Jeroboam's reign in Israel."

- 1 Kings 15:9: "Asa began to rule over Judah in the twentieth year of Jeroboam's reign in Israel."

At first glance, Abijah seems to have reigned only two years, but 2 Chronicles 13:2 clarifies:

"He (Abijah) reigned in Jerusalem for three years."

This contradiction is resolved by recognizing that Abijah served one year as coregent alongside Rehoboam before ruling alone.

Abijah of Judah (936t – 933 Elul)

For reference: Ussher's dates – 958 to 956 BCE; Thiele's dates – 911 to 910 BCE

In Jeroboam's eighteenth year, Abijah ascended to Judah's throne, ruling three years in Jerusalem (2 Chronicles 13:1–2). As noted above, he likely served as coregent with Rehoboam from 936 to 935 BCE, then as sole king from 935 to 933 BCE.

Although Abijah's reign was brief, his determination to reunite the two kingdoms was unwavering. His military campaigns against Jeroboam's larger forces were impressive, significantly weakening Israel's strength during Jeroboam's remaining years.

Asa of Judah (933t to 892 Elul)

For reference: Ussher's dates – 956 to 915 BCE; Thiele's dates – 911 to 870 BCE

The timeline of the Judeo-Israelite monarchies, especially during King Asa's reign, reveals important links between the two dynasties. According to 1 Kings 15:9, Asa began to rule Judah in the twentieth year of Jeroboam, king of Israel. He reigned forty-one years and died around age sixty, as noted in 2 Chronicles 16:13. His reign overlapped with six Israelite kings: Nadab, Baasha, Elah, Zimri, Omri, and Ahab.

Notably, the start of Asa's reign serves as a reference point for six of the nineteen Israelite kings who ruled during the Divided Kingdom. While this might suggest a simplified timeline, aligning each cross-reference demands careful attention to the broader historical context.

During Asa's reign, conflict with Baasha of Israel intensified. Baasha posed a serious threat, leading to the construction of the fortified city of Ramah near Jerusalem. In response, Asa sought help from Ben-Hadad, king of the Arameans, who attacked northern Israelite towns like Ijon, Dan, and Abel Beth Maachah (1 Kings 15:16–22). Ultimately, Ramah came under Judah's control.

Baasha's aggression was triggered by a defection of people from Ephraim,

Manasseh, and Simeon to Asa, who "recognized that the Lord was with him" (2 Chronicles 15:9). Yet 2 Chronicles 16:1 states:

"In the thirty-sixth year of Asa king of Judah, Baasha king of Israel went up against Judah and built Ramah to block all entrances to Judah."

"And Baasha king of Israel went up against Judah, and built Ramah, that he might not suffer any to go out or come in to Asa king of Judah." 1 Kings 15:17

This can be confusing, as Baasha's reign lasted only twenty-four years and he had died before Asa's thirty-sixth year. Many scholars suggest the Hebrew word for "reign" here might better be rendered "kingdom," referring to the broader political entity. Thus, the verse could read:

"In the thirty-sixth year of the kingdom (since the division in 952 BCE), during Asa's reign, Baasha attacked Judah and built Ramah."

This interpretation places Ramah's construction around early 916 BCE, soon after the defections in late 918 BCE. Baasha likely built Ramah in the middle of his reign.

Just as Rehoboam abdicated near the end of his reign, Baasha also stepped down in favor of his son Nadab. In an ironic twist, Nadab met the same fate as Elah. Baasha had murdered Elah to found his dynasty, and similarly, Zimri murdered Nadab to seize power. However, Zimri's reign would be short-lived.

Nadab of Israel (932n – 930 Adar)

For reference: Ussher's dates – 954 to 953 BCE; Thiele's dates – 910 to 909 BCE

Nadab's reign is complicated by the Biblical timeline's compression. Scribes condensed extensive records, omitting many details that must be deduced. According to 1 Kings 15:25, Nadab reigned two years. Some assume his reign began in Asa's second year, but commentators argue he ruled only one year, killed in Asa's third year. Both Ussher and Thiele assign him a one-year reign.

Jeroboam I was still alive when Nadab became king, adding complexity. Nadab likely served as coregent during Jeroboam's final year. Scripture states Nadab reigned two years, suggesting he ruled as vice-regent before his sole reign. However, conventions exclude vice-regencies from total reign lengths. Thus, Nadab's coregency began two years before his death, with sole reign starting after Jeroboam's abdication. Jeroboam's final year counts as part of his reign despite stepping down.

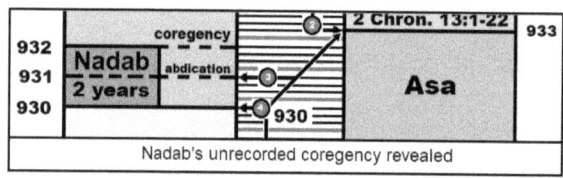
Nadab's unrecorded coregency revealed

This chart visually clarifies this chronology. While unfamiliar to some readers, this pattern is not unique—Elah's reign two decades later shows a similar abdication. Abdications were rare but did occur, as with

Jehoshaphat, who handed the throne to his son Joram while still alive.

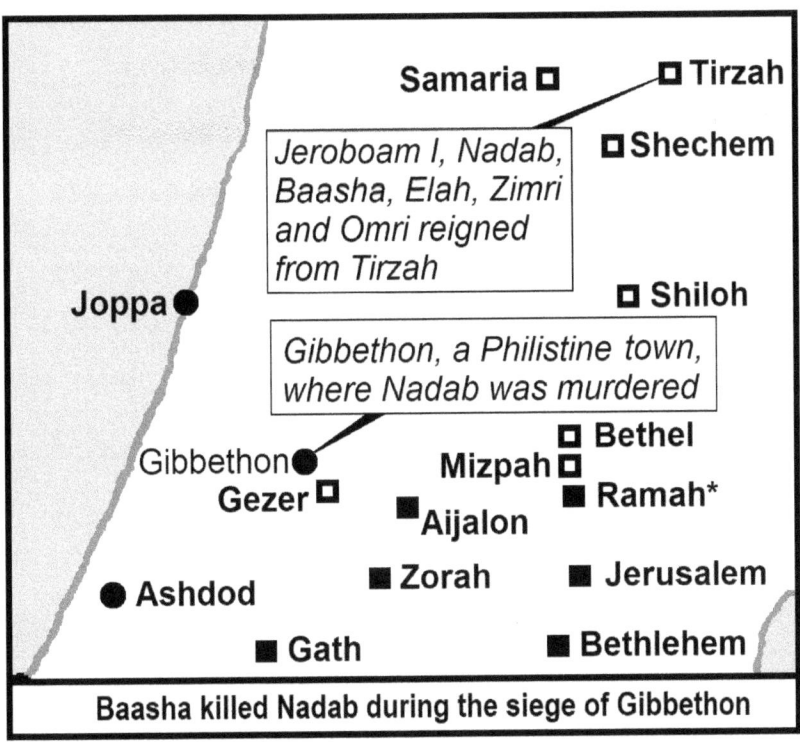

Jeroboam I, Nadab, Baasha, Elah, Zimri and Omri reigned from Tirzah

Gibbethon, a Philistine town, where Nadab was murdered

Baasha killed Nadab during the siege of Gibbethon

In his second year, Nadab attempted to expand Israel's territory by besieging Gibbethon, a Philistine town near the southern boundary at Gezer.

However, Baasha from Issachar thwarted this ambition by assassinating Nadab and seizing the throne during Asa's third year. 1 Kings 15:29–30 records:

"Baasha immediately slaughtered all the descendants of King Jeroboam, so that not one member of the royal family was left, just as the Lord had promised through the prophet Ahijah from Shiloh. This was because Jeroboam had provoked the anger of the Lord by his sins and the sins he led Israel to commit." (NLT)

The "sins of Jeroboam" appear seventeen times in Kings, describing the widespread idolatry promoted by Israel's kings. Details appear in the section on Jeroboam.

Baasha of Israel (930n – 906 Adar)

For reference: Ussher's dates – 953 to 930 BCE; Thiele's dates – 909 to 886 BCE

In Asa's third year as king of Judah, Baasha became king of Israel, ruling for twenty-four years from Tirzah (1 Kings 15:33). Asa, noted for religious reforms, allied with Ben-Hadad I of Damascus against Baasha.

Baasha's reign mirrors Jeroboam I's in that he appointed his son Elah as coregent before stepping down.

Both sets of rulers exhibit a recurring pattern of violent succession. After Jeroboam I died, Baasha killed Nadab to seize the throne. Similarly, Elah was murdered by Zimri following Baasha's death. The Bible records:

"In the twenty-sixth year of Asa king of Judah, Elah the son of Baasha began to reign over Israel... for a period of two years" (1 Kings 16:8).

This places the start of Elah's reign during Baasha's twenty-third year.

Zimri assassinated Elah and took the throne during Asa's twenty-seventh year—just one year after Elah became king. The account states:

"Zimri went in and smote him [Elah]... and reigned in his stead" (1 Kings 16:10, 15).

Elah ruled for two years before being killed (1 Kings 16:8). This succession mirrors Nadab's situation, where Elah served as coregent for two years before Baasha's death. After Baasha abdicated, Elah became sole king.

God's judgment on Baasha was delivered through the prophet Jehu son of Hanani:

"I lifted you out of the dust to make you ruler of my people Israel, but you have followed the evil example of Jeroboam. You have provoked my anger by causing my people Israel to sin. So now I will destroy you and your family, just as I destroyed the descendants of Jeroboam son of Nebat. The members of Baasha's family who die in the city will be eaten by dogs, and those who die in the field will be eaten by vultures." (1 Kings 16:1–4, NLT)

Elah of Israel (908n – 906 Adar)

For reference: Ussher's dates – 930 to 929 BCE; Thiele's dates – 886 to 885 BCE

In Asa's twenty-sixth year over Judah, Elah, Baasha's son, ascended the throne of Israel in Tirzah, reigning for two years (1 Kings 16:8). His two-year reign overlapped Baasha's final years: Elah initially served as coregent before becoming sole monarch after Baasha's abdication. It's important to note that an abdicated king retained the title without executive power.

Elah's coregency lasted one year; upon Baasha's abdication, Elah became sole king but reigned less than a year before Zimri assassinated him. Elah is credited with two years on the throne due to regnal counting conventions.

The Bible offers little on Elah's achievements. It does record that Elah was drinking at a high official's house when Zimri, commander of half the royal chariots, killed him. Zimri then slaughtered all male members of Baasha's family, including distant relatives and associates.

Zimri of Israel (906n, 7 days)

For reference: Ussher's date – 929 BCE; Thiele's date – 885 BCE

1 Kings 16:10 and 15 recount that Zimri killed Elah during Asa's twenty-seventh year and reigned for only seven days in Tirzah. His coronation likely took place in Nisan, fitting the Hebrew coronation calendar.

Many readers might assume Zimri ruled seven days after killing Elah and eliminating Baasha's family. However, the timeline is more subtle. Zimri probably waited for Baasha's natural death before assassinating Elah. He likely struck late in the regnal year, or early in the coronation month, enabling an immediate coronation.

Meanwhile, most of the Israelite army was besieging the Philistine town of Gibbethon in the south. Zimri's swift, quiet coronation aimed to present a fait accompli.

The army, however, rejected this betrayal. They appointed Omri to lead their opposition, abandoning the Gibbethon siege to march on Tirzah. Facing defeat, Zimri retreated to the palace citadel, set it on fire, and took his own life (1 Kings 16:18).

Typically, a new king was crowned by month's end, but two rival claimants emerged: Omri and Tibni, plunging Israel into a civil war that lasted nearly four years.

Ironically, within twenty-four years, the Israelite army twice besieged Gibbethon—both times interrupted by a high-ranking military leader's assassination of their king.

The First Civil War in Israel (906 – 902 BCE)

The biblical narrative in 1 Kings describes Israel's First Civil War between 906 and 902 BCE. It began with Zimri's assassination of King Elah, prompting the army to select Omri as their new king (1 Kings 16:16).

A rivalry quickly formed between Omri and Tibni, splitting Israelite loyalties (1 Kings 16:21). After several years of conflict, Omri defeated Tibni, who died, solidifying Omri's reign (1 Kings 16:22).

After Tibni's death, Omri's rule was uncontested. The text says:

"In the thirty and first year of Asa king of Judah began Omri to reign over Israel, twelve years…" (1 Kings 16:23).

This means Omri's undisputed reign began four years after the civil war started.

The conflict lasted at least three years and a few months but less than four. Omri's twelve-year reign officially began in 902 BCE, following Tibni's death.

The Interregnum Controversy:

Those who oppose the idea of interregnum periods in the Divided Kingdom generally align with Thiele's reasoning. He argues that the Old Testament provides no evidence of any interregnum in Israel or Judah. According to Thiele, a nation cannot exist without a king, and the presence of multiple claimants to the throne during political unrest does not imply a pause in kingship.

Thiele cautions that inserting imagined interregna into the Hebrew kings' timeline leads to confusion and discrepancies, particularly in the lengthy chronologies proposed by Ussher and others. He emphasizes that such hypothetical gaps should only be introduced with strong, corroborating evidence, warning that otherwise they risk distorting the true historical timeline. Thiele is especially critical of Ussher's view, which posits two significant interregna lasting twelve and nine years, respectively.

Questions About Omri's Reign

There remains some debate about the exact moment Omri came to power. Some scholars suggest he became king only after the civil war ended and following the death of his rival, Tibni. It is possible the military recognized Omri as king during the conflict, yet he was never officially crowned while the war was ongoing. The length of his reign is thus counted from his formal coronation.

Additional evidence helps clarify this issue. The following point illustrates the final conclusion.

Septuagint Verses That Solidify Omri's Dates

Edwin Thiele acknowledged the textual differences between the Masoretic Text

(MT) and the Septuagint (LXX) versions of 1 Kings 16:28–29. Although he ultimately dismissed the Septuagint reading, it provides two alternative cross-references that complement rather than contradict the Masoretic Text. These alternatives help establish a more precise chronology for the period.

To illustrate this, consider the two textual versions side by side (numbers refer to MT cross-references; the Septuagint figures are marked with "a" and "b"):

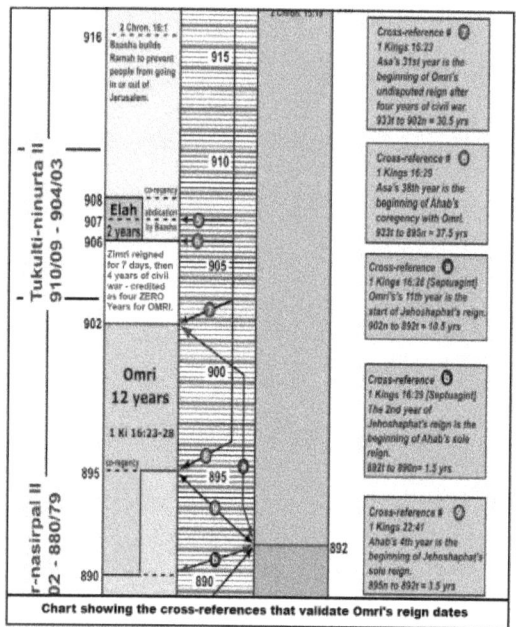

Chart showing the cross-references that validate Omri's reign dates

King James Version (MT):

"So Omri slept with his fathers, and was buried in Samaria: and Ahab his son reigned in his stead. And in the thirty and eighth year of Asa king of Judah began Ahab the son of Omri to reign over Israel: and Ahab the son of Omri reigned over Israel in Samaria twenty and two years."

Septuagint version (LXX):

"And Ambri [Omri] slept with his fathers, and is buried in Samaria; and Achaab [Ahab] his son reigns in his stead. And in the eleventh year of Ambri [Omri] Josaphat [Jehoshaphat] the son of Asa reigns,… In the second year of Josaphat [Jehoshaphat] king of Juda(h), Achaab [Ahab] son of Ambri [Omri] reigned over Israel in Samaria twenty-two years."

The Septuagint explicitly states that Jehoshaphat began his reign during the eleventh year of Omri's rule. This corresponds to approximately 10.5 years before 892 BCE, placing the start of Omri's undisputed reign around 902 BCE. This alignment offers a clear resolution and effectively closes the investigation.

CHAPTER 5

Omri of Israel (902n – 890 Adar)

For reference: Ussher's dates – 929 to 918 | Thiele's dates – 885 to 874

Most scholars agree that the civil war lasted four years before Omri was able to eliminate Tibni and claim the crown. However, E. R. Thiele offers a different timeline, calculating Omri's rivalry with Tibni to span eight years, with Omri reigning alone from 880 to 874 BCE—a total of fourteen years. This conflicts with 1 Kings 16:25, which states Omri reigned for twelve years. This discrepancy is often attributed to the complexities of the non-accession year dating system.

The biblical record provides few details about Omri's accomplishments but does comment sharply on his character: "But Omri did what was evil in the Lord's sight, even more than any of the kings before him" (1 Kings 16:25, NLT). Archaeological evidence, however, sheds more light on his reign—most notably the Moabite Mesha Stele, which attests to Omri's territorial expansion into northern Moab, east of the Jordan River. The stele recounts Moab's subjugation during Omri's rule, highlighting Israel's growing regional power.

During his reign, Omri extended Israelite territory into northern Moab and fostered strong diplomatic ties with Judah. He also secured an alliance with Sidon through intermarriage between the two royal courts. Yet, despite these successes, tensions were mounting to the northeast with the Kingdom of Aram and the rising Assyrian empire—pressures that would intensify under his son Ahab.

According to 1 Kings 16:23–24, "He reigned twelve years in all, six of them in Tirzah. Then Omri bought the hill now known as Samaria from its owner, Shemer, for 150 pounds of silver. He built a city on it and called the city Samaria in honour of Shemer." In modern terms, 150 pounds of silver would be roughly equivalent to USD 80,000 (2025 values).

In the Bible, Tirzah served as a capital city of the Northern Kingdom of Israel before Samaria became the main capital. It was the capital during the reigns of Jeroboam I, Baasha, Elah, Zimri, and Omri (who later moved the capital to Samaria).

The site of Tirzah is identified as Tell el-Farah.

After Zimri set fire to the palace at Tirzah, Omri continued to reign there for six years before constructing a new capital, which he named Samaria. One year after beginning construction, Omri appointed his son Ahab as coregent—likely a strategic move in anticipation of escalating conflict with the Arameans.

Ahab of Israel (895 – 873 BC)

For reference: Ussher's dates – 918 – 897 BC | Thiele's dates – 874 – 853 BC

Ahab's name is infamous through the ages, forever intertwined with his foreign queen, Jezebel—whose legacy has come to embody the archetype of the power-hungry, violent, and promiscuous woman. Jezebel was the daughter of Ethbaal, priest-king of the Phoenician coastal cities Tyre and Sidon. A devoted worshiper of Baal and a woman of formidable will, she persuaded Ahab to introduce Baal worship into Israelite religious life. Her primary devotion was to Baal Hammon, also known as Baal Melkart, a nature deity linked to the Greek Heracles.

In his initial confrontation with the prophet Elijah, Ahab's religious syncretism is revealed; he worshipped multiple gods within the Baal pantheon. As 1 Kings 18:18 (KJV) states, "...ye have forsaken the commandments of the Lord, and thou hast followed Baalim." The plural 'Baalim' suggests devotion not to a single deity but a group including El, Asherah, Anat, Astarte, Yam, Mot, Resheph, Dagon, Kothar, and Shapshu. Baal worship involved agricultural rites, sexual immorality, and child sacrifice—practices sharply opposed to Yahweh worship. Moloch, explicitly associated with child sacrifice, was considered an aspect of Baal but not identical to him.

The Kurkh Monolith describes the Battle of Qarqar and confirms the participation of King Ahab of Israel.

Child sacrifice was commonly practiced in hopes of securing abundant crops or other blessings. One striking example from Ahab's reign involves Hiel of Bethel, who rebuilt Jericho. According to 1 Kings 16:34a (NLT), "It was during his reign that Hiel... laid its foundations; it cost him the life of his oldest son, Abiram. And when he completed it and set up its gates, it cost him the life of his youngest son, Segub." Ancient Hebrew scribal tradition emphasizes this grim toll: "He killed his oldest son when he laid its foundations, and he killed his youngest son when he set up its gates."

There remains debate about Athaliah's lineage—whether she was the daughter of Ahab and Jezebel or of Omri. 2 Kings 8:18 clarifies: "But Jehoram (of Judah) followed the example of the kings of Israel and was as wicked as King Ahab, for he had married one of Ahab's daughters" (NLT). Meanwhile, 2 Chronicles 22:2

describes Athaliah as a daughter of Omri, though the Hebrew term *bath* (בַּת), commonly translated as "daughter," can also mean granddaughter or other female descendant.

During Ahab's reign, peace was maintained with Jehoshaphat of Judah, solidified through the marriage of Ahab's daughter to Jehoshaphat's son (2 Chronicles 18:1). However, this alliance bore significant consequences for Judah in later years, as Athaliah's influence proved detrimental.

After some years, Jehoshaphat journeyed to Samaria to visit Ahab. During this visit, Ahab proposed an alliance to wage war against the King of Aram to recapture Ramoth-gilead. After discussions and consultations with Ahab's prophets—who eagerly endorsed the plan—Jehoshaphat sought the counsel of Micaiah, the son of Imlah, who gave a starkly contrary warning. Despite Micaiah's caution, Jehoshaphat agreed to join the campaign, largely persuaded by Ahab's urgings. This decision nearly cost Jehoshaphat his life, as the King of Aram specifically targeted Ahab for death. On the battlefield, Jehoshaphat was the only king openly wearing royal robes, while Ahab disguised himself. As prophesied, Ahab was mortally wounded and died at sunset.

The two kings had long planned this war and were acutely aware of its dangers. To prepare for a smooth transition in case of death, both appointed their sons as vice-regents. These coronations took place during the New Year celebrations: Tishri 875 BCE for Jehoram of Judah and Nisan 874 BCE for Jehoram of Israel.

At that time, Ahab had already made his eldest son, Ahaziah, coregent. Unfortunately, during Ahaziah's first year, a severe accident left him bedridden and unlikely to recover. For a brief period, Israel was governed by three kings simultaneously: Ahab as the reigning monarch, Ahaziah as coregent, and Jehoram as vice-regent.

Before his fatal campaign at Ramoth-gilead, Ahab had participated in a coalition against Shalmaneser III of Assyria at the battle of Qarqar in 875/874 BCE. This campaign marked Ahab's final regnal year before his death. His son Ahaziah survived him only by a few months, as evidenced by records of his attempts to conduct affairs with Jehoshaphat (1 Kings 22:49).

To assign Ahab his final regnal year, he must have lived past the end of Nisan 875 BCE. Ahaziah, however, did not survive to his coronation as sole king in Nisan 874 BCE; instead, his brother Joram (also known as Jehoram) succeeded to the throne.

Jehoshaphat of Judah (892t – 867 Elul)
For reference: Ussher's dates – 914 to 889 | Thiele's dates – 872 to 848

Jehoshaphat ascended to the throne of Judah at age 35 and ruled for 25 years. He was noted for his efforts to maintain amicable relations with the kings of Israel. Due to a lack of enthusiasm for direct rule, he delegated much of his authority to his son Jehoram (also called Joram).

Historian Edwin Thiele points out chronological difficulties involving Jehoshaphat and the Israelite kings. Specifically, he notes contradictions concerning when Joram, son of Ahab, and Jehoram, son of Jehoshaphat, began their reigns. Thiele speculates that Jehoram of Judah may have started his rule either before or after Joram of Israel, suggesting that Jehoshaphat and his successor may have ruled simultaneously for some time. To clarify these overlapping timelines, a detailed chronological chart has been produced.

The names Joram and Jehoram are interchangeable. Therefore, during this era, when Joram/Jehoram of Israel interacted with Joram/Jehoram of Judah, distinguishing between them requires attention to their kingdom affiliations. Two scriptural references link the beginning of Joram/Jehoram of Israel's reign to the start of Jehoram of Judah's reign—one occurring before Joram of Israel's accession, the other after. Thiele is not alone in grappling with these conflicting verses:

"So Ahaziah died, just as the Lord had promised through Elijah. Since Ahaziah did not have a son to succeed him, his brother Joram became the next king. This took place in the second year of the reign of Jehoram, son of Jehoshaphat, king of Judah." (2 Kings 1:17, NLT)

"And in the fifth year of Joram, the son of Ahab king of Israel, Jehoshaphat being then king of Judah, Jehoram, the son of Jehoshaphat king of Judah, began to reign." (2 Kings 8:16, KJV)

In Tishri 875 BCE, Joram/Jehoram of Judah was crowned vice-regent, anticipating the joint war effort between his father Jehoshaphat and Ahab of Israel against Aram. Ordinarily, the title of vice-regent was largely ceremonial, conferring little real power. Yet cross-references show that vice-regencies rarely serve as chronological markers, unlike coregencies where the coregent exercises full kingly authority. In this case, Jehoshaphat appears to have granted Joram/Jehoram authority beyond a typical vice-regent's, allowing him to wield full regal power. This makes the instance unique, as it stands as the only recorded vice-regency used as a reference point. Joram of Israel's vice-regency may have been used as a reference point because the reigns of the two Joram/Jehorams were bound together through the agreement of Ahab and Jehoshaphat to simultaneously appoint their respective sons to vice-regencies.

By Tishri 873 BCE, Joram/Jehoram of Israel ascended the throne following the deaths of his father Ahab and brother Ahaziah in 874 BCE. His coronation then served as the reference for Jehoram of Judah's sole reign beginning in Tishri 869 BCE, likely following Jehoshaphat's abdication or withdrawal from power, perhaps due to illness. Notably, 2 Kings 8:16 confirms Jehoshaphat was still king when his son began to reign, indicating a possible two-year overlap.

Throughout his reign, Jehoshaphat engaged in various conflicts with neighboring nations. While his intentions seemed sincere, his attempts at cooperation with Israel's royal house sometimes proved ill-advised.

Ahaziah of Israel (875n – 873 Adar)

For reference: Ussher's dates – 898 to 897 | Thiele's dates – 853 to 852

By Ahaziah's reign, the kings of Israel—whose kingdom had increasingly come to be known as Samaria since Ahab's time—had solidified a reputation for embracing evil practices. The biblical account of Ahaziah's brief rule is particularly harsh.

"Ahaziah, son of Ahab, began to rule over Israel in the seventeenth year of King Jehoshaphat's reign in Judah. He reigned in Samaria for two years. But he did what was evil in the Lord's sight, following the example of his father and mother and the example of Jeroboam, son of Nebat, who had led Israel to sin. He served Baal and worshipped him, provoking the anger of the Lord, the God of Israel, just as his father had done." (1 Kings 22:51–53, NLT)

Not only did Ahaziah continue the sins of Jeroboam, but he also followed his father and mother in Baal worship. The Scriptures mention Ahab's wickedness twice within two verses, while Jezebel stands alone in the Hebrew Bible as the only person explicitly criticized for the example she set as a mother.

Ahaziah's role in the dynasty that began with Omri was shaped by the joint military effort between Ahab and Jehoshaphat to reclaim Ramoth-gilead. Both kings promoted their eldest sons—Ahaziah in Israel and Joram (also Jehoram) in Judah—to coregent and vice-regent, respectively. These coronations were celebrated during their kingdoms' respective New Year festivals: Ahaziah in Nisan and Joram/Jehoram in Tishri.

However, Ahaziah's fortunes soon took a drastic turn. According to 2 Kings 1:2 (KJV), "Ahaziah fell down through a lattice in his upper chamber that was in

Samaria and was sick." The Hebrew word *sebakah*, translated as "lattice," can also mean balustrade or railing. His fall from the upper chamber onto a hard stone or marble floor resulted in serious injuries.

The story continues as Ahaziah sends messengers to inquire of Baalzebub, the god of Ekron, whether he would recover. These messengers are intercepted by the prophet Elijah, who delivers a harsh message. Ahaziah sends a captain and fifty men twice to arrest Elijah, but each time, a supernatural intervention prevents them. On the third attempt, the captain pleads for his life and his men's, asking Elijah to come with them to the king. Elijah complies and, upon seeing Ahaziah, declares: "This is what the Lord says: Why did you send messengers to Baal-zebub, the god of Ekron, to ask whether you will recover? Is there no God in Israel to answer your question? Therefore, because you have done this, you will never leave the bed you are lying on; you will surely die." (2 Kings 1:16, NLT)

These events unfolded during Ahaziah's first year as coregent, around 875/874 BCE. Because of Ahaziah's incapacitation and Elijah's prophecy, Ahab prudently appointed Joram/Jehoram as vice-regent the following year. It became clear that Ahaziah would not live long enough to be crowned sole king, leaving Joram/Jehoram as the only viable successor.

Addressing Chronological Hiccups

For readers following the narrative from 1 Kings 22 through 2 Kings 1, the editors who compiled the Books of Kings appear to have arranged events non-chronologically. They often recorded later occurrences before earlier ones, creating challenges for historians and preachers striving to present a coherent timeline.

Much of 1 Kings 22 details events leading to the coalition between Ahab and Jeroboam and their battle with Aram at Ramoth-gilead, which resulted in Ahab's death.

"So Ahab slept with his fathers, and Ahaziah his son reigned in his stead." (1 Kings 22:40) Ahab died in 874 BCE. The next verse leaps back to 892 BCE: "And Jehoshaphat the son of Asa began to reign over Judah in the fourth year of Ahab king of Israel." (1 Kings 22:41)

"Then said Ahaziah the son of Ahab unto Jehoshaphat, 'Let my servants go with thy servants in the ships.' But Jehoshaphat would not." (1 Kings 22:49) This exchange occurred after Ahab's death, dating it to 874/73 BCE.

"And Jehoshaphat slept with his fathers, and was buried with his fathers in the city of David his father: and Jehoram his son reigned in his stead." (1 Kings 22:50) Jehoshaphat died in 867 BCE.

"Ahaziah the son of Ahab began to reign over Israel in Samaria the seventeenth year of Jehoshaphat king of Judah, and reigned two years over Israel." (1 Kings 22:51) Ahaziah's coregency began in 875 BCE.

"Then Moab rebelled against Israel after the death of Ahab." (2 Kings 1:1) The rebellion likely occurred in 874/73 BCE.

"And Ahaziah fell down through a lattice in his upper chamber that was in Samaria …" (2 Kings 1:2) This took place during Ahaziah's first year, 875/74 BCE.

In summary, these sixteen verses shift erratically between 874, 892, 874/73, 867, 875, and back to 874/73 and 875/74 BCE. This discontinuity suggests the redactor was interrupted during compilation, preventing a strict chronological sequence. Casual readers—and even some scholars—may easily misunderstand the timeline. The prevailing scholarly model suggests Azariah's two-year coregency overlapped the final two years of Ahab's reign.

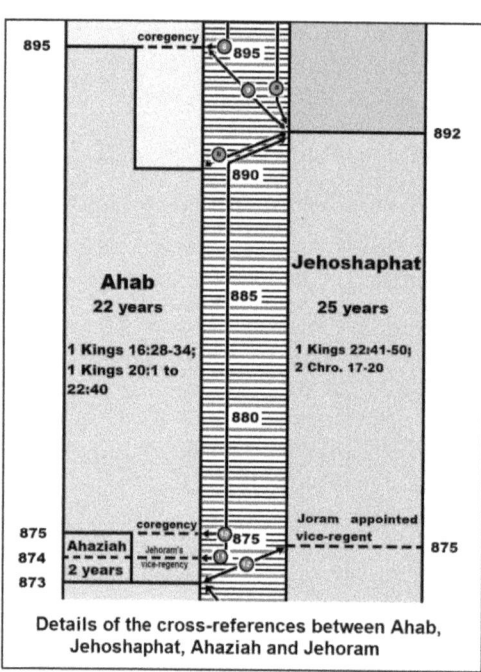

Details of the cross-references between Ahab,
Jehoshaphat, Ahaziah and Jehoram

To clearly illustrate the timeline for this period, it is crucial to closely examine both the chart and the supporting scriptures. At the top of the chart, a cross-reference marked '9' links the beginning of Ahab's reign with the start of Jehoshaphat's reign. This connection is grounded in 1 Kings 22:41, which states, "And Jehoshaphat the son of Asa began to reign over Judah in the fourth year of Ahab, king of Israel." Visually, this relationship on the chart corresponds to a span of approximately three years and six months, providing a key anchor point for understanding the overlapping timelines of these two monarchs.

The cross-reference marked '10' connects the beginning of Jehoshaphat's reign to the start of Ahaziah's. The relevant scripture is 1 Kings 22:51: "Ahaziah the son of Ahab began to reign over Israel in Samaria in the seventeenth year of Jehoshaphat king of Judah, and reigned for two years over Israel." This period spans sixteen years and six months.

Starting from Ahab's reign, the timeline breaks down as follows: three years and six months until Jehoshaphat begins to reign, followed by another sixteen years and six months until Ahaziah ascends the throne—totaling twenty years into Ahab's twenty-two-year reign. Since Ahaziah ruled for two years, his entire reign occurred within Ahab's lifetime, marking it as a coregency. Although Ahaziah held sole reign after Ahab's death, he died before the next potential coronation date in Nisan, at which point Joram/Jehoram was crowned king.

Because of the impending war with Aram, Joram/Jehoram was appointed vice-regent. The calculations that identify 874 BCE as the start of his reign are similar to those used for Ahaziah's coregency with Ahab. Instead of beginning to rule in Jehoshaphat's seventeenth year, Joram/Jehoram started his reign in Jehoshaphat's eighteenth year. This is confirmed by 2 Kings 3:1: "Now Jehoram the son of Ahab began to reign over Israel in Samaria in the eighteenth year of Jehoshaphat king of Judah, and reigned for twelve years." Given Ahaziah was already coregent with Ahab, vice-regent was the only available position for Joram/Jehoram, though he exercised power beyond what the title typically implied—much like Jehoram of Judah, who also wielded significant influence. Both vice-regencies left a lasting historical impact due to their extraordinary authority.

Jehoram of Israel (873n – 861n Adar)

For reference: Ussher's dates – 897 to 885 | Thiele's dates – 852 to 841

Jehoram, son of Ahab, ascended the throne of Israel in Samaria during the eighteenth year of Jehoshaphat's reign over Judah, ruling for twelve years (2 Kings 3:1). He was recognized as vice-regent in 874 BCE and officially began his reign in 873 BCE following the deaths of his father Ahab and brother Ahaziah, who both died in the same year.

In 2 Kings 9:1–27, the prophet Elisha sends a messenger to anoint Jehu as the next king of Israel, signaling a dramatic transition of power. Jehu then travels to Jezreel and kills both Jehoram of Israel and Ahaziah, the visiting king of Judah. These two kings were connected through their familial ties to two of the most reviled women of the era: Jehoram was the son of Jezebel, while Ahaziah of Judah was married to Jehoram's sister, Athaliah. Both women were influential promoters of Baal worship and had pressured the kings of their respective nations to adopt Baal as their god.

Regarding Ahaziah of Judah, two accounts describe his rise to power, likely reflecting two separate coronations spaced about a year apart. The first may have been a coregency or a sole reign initiated by his father stepping aside or abdicating, while the second marked his official crowning as sole king after his father's death. Historical records show no second year of reign for Ahaziah, suggesting he died shortly after becoming sole king—probably early in the month of Tishri.

Jehoram of Israel was killed by Jehu and Ahaziah of Judah was mortally wounded by Jehu during their meeting, with both deaths occurring in Tishri of 862 BCE. Jehoram is credited with the remainder of that regnal year, ending in 861 BCE, having already ruled six months of his final year. These events have implications for the Assyrian inscriptions of Shalmaneser III, specifically the Kurkh Stele (dated to his sixth year) and the Black Obelisk (dated to his eighteenth year). These inscriptions correspond reliably to 874/873 BCE—marking Ahab's last year—and 862/861 BCE—indicating Jehu's first year. These dates differ by twenty-one years from those proposed by Thiele (853 and 841 BCE). This study argues that this discrepancy can be reconciled by reinstating the period of Queen Shammu-ramat's reign—an Assyrian queen who ruled from 830/829 to 810/809 BCE—a reign previously thought to have been erased from history.

CHAPTER 6

Joram (Jehoram) of Judah (870t – 862 Elul)

For reference: Ussher – vr. 893 r. 889 d. 886 | Thiele – vr. 853 r. 848 d. 841

Jehoram was the eldest of seven brothers, who included Azariah, Jehiel, Zechariah, Azariahu, Michael, and Shephatiah. Jehoshaphat, their father, had provided well for all of them, even giving them fortified towns. Jehoram became king because he was the eldest. After ascending to the throne, he ordered the execution of his brothers and other high-ranking officials (2 Chron. 22:2–4). His wife, a daughter of Ahab and Jezebel of Israel, influenced his actions and led him to follow their wicked ways.

At the end of his eight-year reign, Jehoram was forty years old, while his heir, Ahaziah, was twenty-two. However, a scribal error in one verse incorrectly states Ahaziah's age as forty-two. The account of Ahaziah's story is one of survival.

In 2 Chronicles 21:16–17 it states:

"Then the Lord stirred up the Philistines and the Arabs, who lived near the Ethiopians, to attack Jehoram. They marched against Judah, broke down its defences, and carried away everything of value in the royal palace, including the king's sons and his wives. Only his youngest son, Ahaziah, was spared" (NLT).

Knowing that Ahaziah was the youngest helps establish a timeline for the peace treaty between Ahab and Jehoshaphat, which included the marriage of Ahab's daughter to Jehoshaphat's son. When Ahaziah claimed the throne in 862 BCE, he was twenty-two years old. However, he was appointed co-regent in 863 BCE due to his father's alarming health issues, introducing an uncertainty factor of one year.

Ahaziah was born in 885 or 884 BCE. Jehoshaphat had ascended to the throne in 892 BCE, roughly seven or eight years before the birth of his youngest grandson.

Jehoshaphat entered into a peace treaty with Ahab very soon after his coronation.

Jehoram's Progression of Power

When Jehoshaphat and Ahab agreed to attempt to recapture Ramoth-gilead, they both appointed their eldest sons to the title of king: Azariah as co-regent to Ahab and Jehoram as vice-regent to Jehoshaphat.

"...Joram [of Israel] became the next king. This took place in the second year of the reign of Jehoram, son of Jehoshaphat, king of Judah" (2 Kings 1:17, NLT).

- 875 BCE: Jehoram of Israel was crowned as vice-regent in Tishri.

- 870 BCE: Initiation of co-regency, marking the beginning of his official reign.

- 869 BCE: Assumption of full kingly authority following Jehoshaphat's abdication.

- 867 BCE: Reign as sole king until the appointment of Ahaziah as co-regent in 863 BCE.

- 862 BCE: His death.

During his reign, the Edomites, who had lived peacefully under the rule of Judah, revolted. Jehoram and his army were surrounded and could only escape under the cover of night. Things were not going well for this king.

While Ahab reigned, the prophet Elijah posed significant challenges to his rule. Elijah also confronted Ahab's son and foretold that he would die. Now, imagine being another evil king on Elijah's list and receiving the following letter.

Elijah the Prophet's Letter to Jehoram

"This is what the Lord, the God of your ancestor David, says: You have not followed the good example of your father, Jehoshaphat, or your grandfather King Asa of

Judah. Instead, you have been as evil as the kings of Israel. You have led the people of Jerusalem and Judah to worship idols, just as King Ahab did in Israel. And you have even killed your own brothers, men who were better than you. So now the Lord is about to strike you, your people, your children, your wives, and all that is yours with a heavy blow. You yourself will suffer from a severe intestinal disease that will worsen each day until your bowels come out" (2 Chron. 21:12–15, NLT).

Shortly after this prophecy, the Philistines and Arabs carried off anything of value from the palace, including his wives and children, except for Ahaziah. During his last two years, Jehoram suffered the prophesied illness, and his final days were debilitating and painful.

"...No one was sorry when he died. They buried him in the City of David, but not in the royal cemetery" (2 Chron. 21:20).

Ahaziah of Judah (863t – 862 Elul)

For reference: Ussher – vr. 887 r. 886 d. 886 | Thiele – vr. 842 r. 841 d. 841

The brief rule of Ahaziah lasted just one year, presenting significant challenges for historians and scholars due to conflicting chronological accounts regarding the start of his reign. These accounts differ by one year despite his single year in power.

The biblical text in 2 Kings provides two distinct references to the beginning of Ahaziah's reign:

"And in the eleventh year of Joram the son of Ahab, Ahaziah began to reign over Judah" (2 Kings 9:29) and *"In the twelfth year of Joram the son of Ahab, king of Israel, Ahaziah the son of Jehoram, king of Judah, began to reign. Ahaziah was twenty-two years old when he began to reign, and he reigned one year in Jerusalem..."* (2 Kings 8:25–26).

Ahaziah was the son of Jehoram, who experienced a prolonged illness lasting two years before his death, which modern medicine might diagnose as a prolapse. Ahaziah received kingly power one year before Jehoram died. It can only have been a coregency, or Jehoram abdicated authority to him. This arrangement accounts for his first coronation.

After Jehoram died, they formally crowned Ahaziah as the sole king during his second coronation. However, Jehu killed him shortly after this event.

In 2 Chronicles 22:3–6, the text describes the events surrounding his death: *"Ahaziah also followed the evil example of King Ahab's family, for his mother encouraged him to do wrong. He did what was evil in the Lord's sight, just as Ahab's family had done. They even became his advisers after the death of his father, leading him to ruin. Following their evil advice, Ahaziah joined Joram, the son of King Ahab of Israel, in his war against King Hazael of Aram at Ramoth-gilead. When the Arameans wounded Joram in battle, he returned to Jezreel to recover from his injuries. Because Joram was wounded, King Ahaziah of Judah went to Jezreel to visit him"* (NLT).

The Scriptures imply that Amaziah did not survive beyond the coronation month of Tishri, although they do not explicitly state this. If he had, they would have credited him with a second year of reign, which would be the case according to the accession method for the accounting of reigns.

The timing indicates that Ahaziah left his army at Ramoth-gilead to attend his coronation in Jerusalem following the death of his father. Upon hearing about Joram of Israel's injuries, he decided to visit his uncle, as Joram was his mother's brother.

Unfortunately for Ahaziah, this visit coincided with Jehu, a general in the Israelite army, being anointed and appointed to carry out judgment against the family of Ahab. When Jehu and his men encountered Ahaziah's entourage, which included family members and officials, they killed them all. Although Ahaziah managed to flee to Samaria, he was ultimately captured and executed. Out of respect for his grandfather Jehoshaphat, they granted him a decent funeral.

Queen Athaliah of Judah (862t – 856 Elul)

For reference: Ussher's dates – 886 to 879 | Thiele's dates – 841 to 835

If a modern-day author of horror tales were searching for the perfect template for an evil queen, the search would need to go no further than Queen Athaliah. As the offspring of two of history's most notorious rulers, Ahab and Jezebel, she married into the Judean royal family to secure a peace treaty. Her toxic influence extended to convincing her husband to kill his six brothers after his coronation in order to eliminate any challenge to his kingship.

The death of Athaliah

Athaliah's husband, Jehoram of Judah, was suffering from an intestinal disease. During this time, their son Ahaziah assumed power, either by co-regency with

Jehoram or through Jehoram's abdication. He ruled for one year before being killed by Jehu. Throughout his brief reign, Athaliah continued to wield significant influence: *"Ahaziah also followed the evil example of King Ahab's family, for his mother encouraged him to do wrong"* (2 Chronicles 22:3, NLT).

"When Athaliah, the mother of King Ahaziah of Judah, learned that her son was dead, she began to destroy the rest of Judah's royal family. But Ahaziah's sister, Jehosheba, the daughter of King Jehoram, took Ahaziah's infant son, Joash, and hid him away from the other royal children, who were about to be killed. She placed Joash and his nurse in a bedroom, successfully keeping him safe from Athaliah's murderous intentions. Joash remained hidden in the Temple of God for six years while Athaliah ruled over the land" (2 Chronicles 22:10–12, NLT).

Although Jehosheba is identified as Ahaziah's sister, she was not Athaliah's daughter. King Joram had other wives, and while all male heirs except for Ahaziah were carried off by the Philistines and the Arabs, he also had daughters from his other wives. As Jehosheba was married to Jehoiada the priest, it is inconceivable that Athaliah, who promoted the worship of Baal, would have permitted any of her daughters to marry a priest of the God of the Hebrews. In 2 Kings 12:1, we see that Joash's mother's name was Zibiah of Beersheba.

Ahaziah died in Tishri, the coronation month, which allowed Athaliah to be crowned before the month ended. She has the distinction of being the sole female monarch during the period of the Divided Kingdom. The following phrase summarizes her historical contribution: *"And Athaliah did reign over the land"* (2 Kings 11:3, KJV).

When Joash was just one year old, Jehosheba hid him in the Temple. Six years later, Jehoiada orchestrated a carefully planned coup and installed Joash as king with military precision.

"And he [Jehoiada] brought forth the king's son, and put the crown upon him, and gave him the testimony; and they made him king, and anointed him; and they clapped their hands, and said, 'God save the king'" (2 Kings 11:12, NLT).

By the time the commotion reached Athaliah, she had already sealed her fate. They escorted her from the Temple because it would have been improper to kill her there: *"And they laid hands on her; and she went by the way by which the horses came into the king's house: and there was she slain... And all the people of the land rejoiced"* (2 Kings 11:16, 20, NLT).

Jehu of Israel (861t – 833 Adar)

For reference: Ussher's dates – 886 to 857 | Thiele's dates – 841 to 814

The Black Obelisk of Shalmaneser III depicts King Jehu of Israel bowing before the Assyrian king.

The mathematics associated with Jehu's reign presents a unique challenge for commentators, as the circumstances that led to his rise to power created a moment of surprise. In 2 Kings 9, the story unfolds of how the prophet Elisha sent a young prophet to Ramoth-gilead, where Jehu was with the army, to anoint him with oil. The prophet declared: *"Thus says the Lord, I have anointed you king over Israel"* (verse 3). He continued: *"You shall strike down the house of Ahab your master, so that I may avenge the blood of My servants the prophets, and the blood of all the*

91

servants of Adonai shed by Jezebel. For the entire house of Ahab will perish, and I will cut off from Ahab every male, slave or free, in Israel. I will make the house of Ahab like the house of Jeroboam, son of Nebat, and like the house of Baasha, son of Ahijah. The dogs will eat Jezebel in the field of Jezreel, and there will be none to bury her" (2 Kings 9:7–10, TOL).

When Jehu's fellow officers learned that he had been anointed king, they quickly spread their cloaks on the bare steps, blew the ram's horn, and shouted, *"Jehu is king!"* These actions—anointing with oil, blowing trumpets, and acknowledging Jehu as king—were all part of the formalities surrounding the crowning of a king.

This event occurred in Tishri, shortly after Ahaziah was crowned the sole king that same month. For Jehu, there was an urgency to act; he needed to move before news of his claim to the throne reached King Jehoram.

The narrative describes how Jehu, accompanied by troops, drove his chariot immediately to Jezreel, where Jehoram was recuperating from his battle wounds while Ahaziah of Judah was visiting him. The two kings came out in their chariots to meet Jehu. An arrow struck Jehoram in the heart, while Azariah fled but was also killed. All of this transpired within a matter of days.

In Israel's tradition, coronations were usually held in the month of Nisan, but the people crowned Jehu in Tishri. In those extraordinary times, this was equivalent to a field promotion. This unusual timing added six months at the beginning of Jehu's reign, resulting in a total reign of twenty-eight and a half years. However, the official record states that "Jehu reigned over Israel from Samaria for twenty-eight years" (2 Kings 10:36). The lengths of reign in Israel generally count from the first day of Nisan, which explains this discrepancy.

The rounding down to twenty-eight years is not unique in Scripture. Consider the reign of King David: "He was thirty years old when he began to reign, and he reigned forty years in all. He had reigned over Judah from Hebron for seven years and six months, and from Jerusalem he reigned over all Israel and Judah for thirty-three years" (2 Samuel 5:4–5, NLT). Although David's total reign was forty and a half years, it has been rounded down to forty years.

The Unique Cross-reference from Jehu's Reign

"In the seventh year of Jehu, Jehoash began to reign..." (2 Kings 12:1, NLT). Shortly after being confirmed as king, Jehu killed Jehoram of Israel and Ahaziah of Judah. Athaliah seized power in Judah and ruled for six years, beginning in the month of Tishri, while her grandson Joash was secretly hidden in the Temple. The Scripture states:

"And he was with her hidden in the house of the Lord six years. And Athaliah reigned over the land. In the seventh year, Jehoiada sent and gathered the rulers over hundreds, along with the captains and the guard, and brought them to him in the house of the Lord. He made a covenant with them, took an oath of them in the house of the Lord, and showed them the king's son" (2 Kings 11:3–4).

Verse 4 is particularly significant with the mention of "the seventh year." The count began in the year 862 BCE, corresponding to Tishri. The end of Athaliah's six-year reign fell on 29 Elul 856 BCE. This date also marked the start of Joash's seventh year of hiding and coincided with the beginning of Jehu's seventh year since his anointing (2 Kings 12:1).

Thus far in this book, we have encountered cross-references involving vice-regencies, coregencies, abdications, and sole reigns. All of these have followed familiar patterns, but now we see an exception. The scribes rounded down the length of Jehu's reign by six months, but they used the early coronation date as a reference for Joash's coronation. Although only a few days or weeks passed between the two events, which totals just over six years, the Scriptures accurately refer to it as the seventh year.

The Importance of Events Between Jehu's Coronation and Joash's Coronation

Jehu had a mandate to "strike down the house of Ahab." He focused solely on achieving that goal, and it was not fully realized until the Judeans killed Athaliah and installed Joash as king. His achievements included the slaughter of the Baal-worshipping kings of Israel and Judah, along with their extended families. His next target was Jezebel, who was staying in Jezreel.

"When Jezebel, the queen mother, heard that Jehu had come to Jezreel, she painted her eyelids and fixed her hair and sat at a window. When Jehu entered the gate of the palace, she shouted at him, 'Have you come in peace, you murderer? You're just like Zimri, who murdered his master!'

Jehu looked up and saw her at the window and shouted, 'Who is on my side?' And two or three eunuchs looked out at him. 'Throw her down!' Jehu yelled. So they threw her out the window, and her blood spattered against the wall and on the horses. And Jehu trampled her body under his horses' hooves" (2 Kings 9:30–33, NLT).

2 Kings 10 tells how Jehu wrote to the leaders of the city of Samaria, who were caretakers for Ahab's seventy sons from numerous wives. When they asked what Jehu wanted, he demanded the heads of Ahab's sons. They were delivered to Jehu in baskets by the following morning.

In the aftermath of Jezebel's death and the demise of Ahab's sons, Jehu undertook significant measures aimed at religious and political reform in Israel. He convened a large assembly that was publicly characterized as a Baal worship service. However, under this pretext, he directed his forces to eliminate the Baal worshippers who had been lured to the event. Following this decisive action, Jehu dismantled the temple of Baal along with its associated idols, effectively signaling a shift away from Baal worship in the region. In a symbolic gesture of transformation, he repurposed the formerly sacred site into a public latrine.

How Jehu's Early Coronation Fits into the Length of Reign Calculations

When Jehu assassinated Jehoram of Israel during his twelfth year of reign, convention dictated that the calculation of his reign counted until the last day of Adar, giving him a full twelve years. Typically, scribes counted the balance of the year leading up to 1 Nisan as the Zero Year for the incoming king's reign, which in this case was Jehu. The accounting of his reign officially began with his coronation month, which was 1 Nisan 861 BCE, even though his coronation had been hastily convened in Tishri 862 BCE.

Interactions with Shalmaneser III of Assyria: The Kurkh Stele and the Black Obelisk

The Assyrian records reveal two significant interactions between the king of Assyria and the king of Israel that the biblical account does not mention. The Kurkh Stele records the events leading up to the Battle of Qarqar, which historians traditionally date to 853 BCE.

This battle involved the Assyrians, led by Shalmaneser III, against a coalition of eleven nations. The monolith lists the enemy combatants, including Ahab of Israel.

The biblical record focuses on Jehu's efforts to eliminate the murderous cult of Baal and the family of Ahab, who supported it. After the seventh year of Jehu's reign, there are no recorded events for the next two decades. However, historical records reference an interaction between Jehu and King Shalmaneser III of Assyria during the eighteenth year of Shalmaneser's reign.

A relief showing King Jehu bowing before King Shalmaneser III is considered the earliest surviving image of a biblical figure. The conventionally accepted date for this event is 841 BCE.

How Thiele Dealt with These Dates

The examination of the Assyrian Eponym Lists provided the dates for the events of 853 and 841 BCE. Thiele believed that the Assyrian record was highly accurate, and his thesis relied on aligning the supposedly precise Assyrian chronology with the biblical timeline. However, Thiele faced a significant challenge: the last year of Ahab and the first year of Jehu seemed to be separated by fourteen years, while the Assyrian records indicated just a twelve-year gap.

Thiele reasoned that after Ahab's death, Ahaziah ruled for two years, followed by Jehoram, who reigned for twelve years. These reign lengths added up to fourteen years, prompting Thiele to employ some creative adjustments. By applying the non-accession system, he subtracted one year from the beginning of Ahaziah's reign and removed a year from the end of Jehoram's reign.

The Calculations Derived from This Book

This book argues that we can derive the absolute timeline for the Divided Kingdom from the data available in the books of Kings and Chronicles. No other external chronology is required, except to establish datum points. Only after fully reconciling the biblical data can synchronisms with the Assyrian timeline be attempted.

The analysis of Ahab's reign reveals that Azariah's two-year reign was a coregency with Ahab, encompassing the last two years of Ahab's reign. Ahab likely died in 874 BCE. Ahaziah died in the same regnal year, 874/873 BCE.

Jehoram, the younger son of Ahab, was crowned in Nisan and assassinated in Tishri 862 BCE. Jehu was crowned immediately in that same month. The period between the last year of Ahab (874) and the first year of Jehu (862) is twelve years, which complies precisely with the Assyrian record.

When we align the Hebrew dates with Assyrian history, we find that the Battle of

Qarqar occurred in 874 BCE, and Shalmaneser III's encounter with Jehu occurred in 862 BCE. One of the explanations for the twenty-one-year discrepancy between the Hebrew and Assyrian figures is the deletion of the reign of Shammu-ramat. A later chapter will address this issue.

Jehoash/Joash of Judah (856 Tishri – 816 Elul)

For reference: Ussher's dates – 879 to 839; Thiele's dates – 835 to 798

In the seventh year of Jehu's reign, Jehoash became king and ruled for forty years in Jerusalem (2 Kings 12:1). His ascent to the throne is particularly noteworthy because he began his reign at just seven years old, having been hidden in the Temple for six years to escape his grandmother Athaliah's murderous intentions.

A significant aspect of Joash's rule was the restoration of the Temple, which was in disrepair. However, by the twenty-third year of his reign, the restoration was still not completed (2 Kings 12:6). To address this, the king secured funding for the project and finished it in the following years. During his reign, Jehoiada, the priest who had preserved his life, guided Joash and helped facilitate his rule.

When Jehoiada died during the second half of Joash's reign, other advisors influenced him to abandon the Temple and promote other practices. Various prophets warned Joash, but he and his advisors ignored them. Towards the end of his reign, Zechariah, a son of Jehoiada the priest, proclaimed a message that was scathing of the state of the nation (2 Chronicles 24:20). The leaders conspired to kill Zechariah, and King Joash ordered his stoning.

Justice was swift, for the Arameans invaded Jerusalem and killed many of the leaders. Joash was left wounded, and two of his servants killed him for treacherously murdering Zechariah, the son of the man who had preserved him from death and guided him for close to forty years.

Two years before his death, Joash appointed his son Amaziah as coregent. This timing corresponds with the beginning of Jehoash of Israel's coregency with his father, Jehoahaz. A careful analysis of the timeline supports this connection. Given the start of Jehoash's reign relative to the death of Joash of Judah, it created a puzzle for which an answer was not immediately apparent. The coregency framework best explains these events and maintains the continuity of the timeline. According to 2 Kings 14:1, Amaziah began his reign in the second year of Joash, the son of Jehoahaz, king of Israel.

Jehoahaz of Israel (833 Nisan – 816 Adar)

For reference: Ussher's dates – 857 to 840; Thiele's dates – 814 to 797

In the twenty-third year of Joash, king of Judah, Jehoahaz, the son of Jehu, began his reign over Israel in Samaria, ruling for seventeen years (2 Kings 13:1). Later, in the thirty-seventh year of Joash's reign in Judah, Jehoash, the son of Jehoahaz, became king of Israel in Samaria.

Jehoahaz's reign started in Joash's twenty-third year, and Jehoash's reign began in Joash's thirty-seventh year. Notably, Jehoash began his reign fourteen years after the start of his father's seventeen-year reign. This timeline strongly suggests that they ruled concurrently during the last three years of Jehoahaz's reign.

During Jehoahaz's reign, Israel faced constant attacks from Hazael and then his son Benhadad of Syria. The situation in Israel became so dire that Jehoahaz, who had followed other gods, "besought the Lord, and the Lord hearkened unto him..." (2 Kings 13:4, KJV). Verse 5 describes the solution: "And the Lord gave Israel a saviour, so that they went out from under the hand of the Syrians, and the children of Israel dwelt in their tents as before."

Historians speculate about the identity of the unnamed saviour. Some believe it was King Adad-nirari III of Assyria, based on Thiele's compressed timeline. Before the end of Jehoahaz's reign, a period of peace ensued. According to Thiele's calculations, the king's reign ended in 797 BCE. Historical records indicate that Adad-nirari III captured Damascus in 796 BCE, following the reign of Jehoahaz.

Assyria had been in conflict with the Arameans since the time of Shalmaneser III, which was a century and a half earlier. Most of King Jehoahaz's reign coincided with the reign of Shammuramat (830/29 to 810/09). Shammuramat, the mother of Adad-nirari III, rose to power through negotiations with high officials and city governors. In exchange for their acceptance of her as Queen Regent, she devolved certain powers to them.

During this transition, Assyria became less militaristic, which allowed other nations to assert themselves in the region. One such power was Aram, which, although closely related to Syria, was a confederation of city states within Syria's boundaries. In the biblical texts, Syria and Aram are often used interchangeably.

A later king of Assyria, almost certainly Tiglath Pileser III, took great care to erase the records of much of Shammuramat's reign. After establishing her position and influence, she worked to restore Assyria's vassal states, which neighboring nations targeted in their quest for power expansion. Aram likely became a primary target for the Assyrians during this time.

The Assyrians sought to reclaim their status as a regional superpower, which Syrian expansionism threatened to undermine. Israel benefited from this realignment of power, with Shammuramat, "The Warrior Queen of Assyria," emerging as the unexpected saviour of Israel.

Jehoash of Israel (819 Nisan to 803 Adar)

For reference: Ussher's dates – 840 to 825; Thiele's dates – 797 to 782

In the thirty-seventh year of Joash's reign in Judah, Jehoash became king of Israel and ruled for sixteen years. He achieved significant military victories, particularly against the Syrians, who had nearly destroyed the nation during his father's reign.

The saviour intervened, disrupting the frequency and intensity of the Syrian attacks (2 Kings 13:4). Under Jehoash's leadership, Israel managed to rebuild its army to the point where it could effectively repel ongoing assaults.

During the final days of the prophet Elisha, Jehoash visited him (2 Kings 13:14–18). Elisha prophesied that he would defeat Syria at Aphek, located on the eastern side of the Sea of Galilee, and foretold three additional victories. Following this, "Jehoash son of Jehoahaz recaptured from Ben-hadad son of Hazael the towns that had been taken from his father, Jehoahaz. Jehoash defeated Ben-hadad on three occasions and recovered the Israelite towns" (2 Kings 13:25, NLT).

Another Unique Cross Reference

Toward the end of his reign, Amaziah, the king of Judah, provoked a war with Israel and suffered a decisive defeat. Amaziah, along with many Judean hostages, was captured and imprisoned. During this time, the Israelite army looted the palace and the Temple in Jerusalem, demolishing six hundred feet of the city's walls (2 Kings 14:14).

There is much speculation regarding the length of Amaziah's imprisonment. There is no evidence for a long period of incarceration. The ten-year term that some commentators have suggested aligns closely to the invented coregency between Jehoash and Jeroboam II.

This situation introduces an unusual cross reference. "King Amaziah of Judah lived for fifteen years after the death of King Jehoash of Israel" (2 Kings 14:17; 2 Chronicles 25:25). Unlike other cross references that typically measure time from a viceregency, coregency, or sole reign to the start of another reign, this one is different. It measures the time between two deaths. Furthermore, instead of referring to "the fifteenth year," this verse specifies "fifteen years."

The emphasis on two deaths suggests a possible connection between them.

Interestingly, 2 Kings 14:19 states, "There was a conspiracy against Amaziah's life in Jerusalem..." This circumstance raises the possibility that Amaziah, even while being held captive, may have played a role in the death of Jehoash.

We can establish a narrower range of dates for the deaths through deduction. According to the conventions regarding the calculation of reign length, Jehoash might have died at any point after the first month of his final regnal year (804/03), while still having that year credited to his reign. In Judah, the latest date that Amaziah could have survived was Tishri in 789 BCE. Fifteen years before that would be Tishri 804 BCE. Therefore, Jehoash died sometime between Iyar and Tishri in 804 BCE.

The challenge for anyone reading the chart lies in the fact that the arrows for cross reference number 21 might move up to six months earlier than their current positions. However, this does not affect the overall timeline.

Amaziah has been quite unprincipled. He launched an unprovoked war against his neighbor, suffered a crushing defeat, and ultimately led to the ruination of his capital. While he was imprisoned, possibly as a tactic to keep an aggressive Judah in check, authorities established a caretaker government. Once released, Amaziah's unscrupulous nature compelled him to install his five year old son as coregent while he sought to evade assassins.

The circumstances surrounding Jehoash's death appeared suspicious, contributing to the ongoing poor relations between the two nations. The assassins tracked down Amaziah in Lachish and killed him.

John Ferris

CHAPTER 7

Amaziah of Judah (818t – 789 Elul)

For reference: Ussher's dates – 839 to 810 | Thiele's dates – 796 to 767

Two years before the assassination of his father, Joash, Amaziah was appointed as coregent. When he became the sole king, one of his early priorities was to execute the servants who had killed his father. Notably, he spared the children of the assassins, following the Mosaic law that states parents should not be punished for the crimes of their children, and vice versa. Amaziah's story serves as a lesson in character, illustrating that listening to God and His prophets leads to success, while following bad counsel results in ruin.

Edom had been under the control of Judah until the reign of King Jehoram, who was Amaziah's great-grandfather. After nearly sixty years, Amaziah planned an attack on Edom. Judah commanded 300,000 elite troops and, to strengthen his forces, he hired 100,000 mercenaries from Israel for a total cost of 7,500 pounds of silver. However, an unnamed prophet warned Amaziah against including the idolatrous Israelites, stating that God would not support the effort if they were involved.

Judah proceeded alone and easily won the conflict, killing 10,000 enemies and capturing another 10,000, whom they then threw off a cliff. Amaziah returned with a significant amount of plunder, including idols that he set up as his personal gods and worshipped.

While Judah was engaged in battle with the Edomites, the Israelite mercenaries returned home in a rage. Although they were allowed to keep their silver, they had likely expected to share in the rich plunder. On their way back to Samaria, they pillaged several Judean towns and murdered 3,000 people. When a prophet came to rebuke King Amaziah, he threatened to kill the prophet. Following this, he called in his advisors to discuss their next steps.

After easily defeating Edom, Amaziah likely received advice to challenge Israel to battle, particularly after Israelite mercenaries pillaged Judean villages. Jehoash of Israel tried to avoid an unnecessary conflict and sent Amaziah a message:

"You are saying, 'I have defeated Edom,' and you are very proud of it. But my advice is to stay at home. Why stir up trouble that will only bring disaster on you and the people of Judah?" (2 Chronicles 25:18, NLT).

During the reign of Jehoahaz of Israel, constant attacks by Syria had significantly weakened the Israelite army, leaving them with only 50 charioteers, 10 chariots, and 10,000 foot soldiers (2 Kings 13:7). However, within a generation, Jehoash managed to rebuild the army to such an extent that he could hire out 100,000 men to Judah. This number, however, was only a portion of Israel's fighting men, who likely outnumbered the 300,000 men available to Amaziah.

Amaziah faced a devastating battle and was captured. The forces of Israel overran Jerusalem and took the treasures from the Temple and the Palace. Demolishers removed a 600-foot section of Jerusalem's wall, leaving the city vulnerable to attacks for many years to come. Furthermore, Amaziah and several high-ranking officials were captured and may have remained as hostages until Jehoash's death.

As mentioned in the section on Jehoash of Israel, the unique cross-reference indicates a connection between the deaths of Jehoash and Amaziah, measuring the time between the two events. Amaziah was ultimately killed by assassins, raising questions about whether Jehoash also died under suspicious circumstances.

Following Amaziah's release, he remained king but became a pariah in his own country due to the devastation his decisions had inflicted upon the nation. Conspiracies against him were rampant, forcing him to move constantly to evade assassination threats. To ensure the continuity of rule in the event of his demise,

Amaziah appointed his son Uzziah as coregent at the young age of five.

Eventually, Amaziah fled to Lachish, where he was caught and killed. The populace then embraced the new king, Uzziah, who was 16 at the time (2 Kings 14:21).

Jeroboam II of Israel (803n – 762 Adar)

For reference: Ussher – vr. 826 r. 815 to 784 | Thiele – vr. 793 r. 782 to 753

During the reign of Jeroboam II, scholars encountered a significant challenge in reconciling the reigns of Jehoash, Jeroboam's father, Amaziah of Judah, and his son Uzziah. In his 1650 publication, Bishop James Ussher assumed that 2 Kings 15:1–2 referred to a single event; however, these verses describe two events separated by 12 years.

To account for this 12-year gap, Ussher introduced an 11-year coregency with his father, Jehoash, which led to an error in his timeline. As a result, he later proposed 12 years of interregnum. Similarly, Thiele made the same significant error, following Ussher's approach by positing an 11-year coregency with Jehoash.

Jeroboam II began his reign over Israel in 803 BCE, which was the fifteenth year of Amaziah's reign in Judah. He ruled for 41 years, making his reign the longest of any king of Israel (2 Kings 12:23). He led Israel to significant prosperity and military success during his reign.

During his reign, the territory controlled by Israel extended north to Hamath, which is approximately 120 miles north of Damascus. Hamath serves as the northernmost point of the Promised Land, as noted in Joshua 13:5.

During Jeroboam's reign, King Ashur-Dan III of Assyria led military campaigns that weakened Syria. The dates for Ashur-Dan's reign are well-documented in ancient history, as the eponym for his ninth year references a solar eclipse, calculated to have occurred on June 15, 763 BCE. His three campaigns against

Syria took place early in his reign.

The Great Earthquake

Amos 1:1 (NLT): "This message was given to Amos, a shepherd from the town of Tekoa in Judah. He received this message in visions two years before the earthquake, when Uzziah was king of Judah and Jeroboam II, the son of Jehoash, was king of Israel."

Although the historian Josephus connects the earthquake with Uzziah being struck down with leprosy, there is no other evidence to support that scenario.

The earthquake was a significant event, with stratigraphic evidence indicating widespread damage occurring around 760 BCE. The estimated magnitude of the quake ranges from 7.8 to 8.2, with its epicentre located in Lebanon. Given that Jeroboam and Uzziah had lengthy reigns overlapping for about 37 years, it has been challenging to pinpoint a specific date for this event.

Assyria was also dramatically impacted, with many cities suffering extensive damage. The eponym records of Ashur-dan III describe his reign as tumultuous, marked by years of plague and civil unrest. Symbolically, their chief god, Shamash, represented by the Sun, was blotted out by a total eclipse during this time. The Assyrian people interpreted this as divine judgment. In the eponym lists, any year marked by the phrase "the king stayed in the land" indicates that there were domestic issues requiring the king's attention.

Each year, Assyrian kings routinely engaged in military campaigns, and Ashur-dan III was no exception. During his first three years, he participated in campaigns, but in his fourth year, he remained in the land. The military campaigns resumed the following year. What caused the king to stay in the land in 768/67 BCE? Could it have been the earthquake that Amos described? This date certainly warrants consideration.

The End of Jeroboam II's Reign

Throughout his reign, Jeroboam maintained friendly relations with his neighbours in Judah. At some point between Uzziah's affliction with leprosy and Jeroboam II's death, Jotham became vice-regent, although the coronation is not recorded, which was common for this period. The title of vice-regent also came with the title of king.

During the period of peace between Israel and Judah, scribes compiled official genealogies. As noted in 1 Chronicles 5:17 (NLT): *"All of these were listed in the genealogical records during the days of King Jotham of Judah and King Jeroboam of Israel."* This verse makes it clear that Jotham held the title of king during Jeroboam's reign, which contradicts the claims made by Ussher and Thiele.

As Jeroboam neared his final days, he may have appointed his son Zechariah as vice-regent, though this remains undocumented. Jeroboam ruled for 41 years, during which the prophets Hosea, Joel, Amos, and Jonah condemned the materialism and selfishness of the Israelite elite.

Azariah (Uzziah) of Judah (800t – 748 Elul)
For reference: Ussher – 810 to 758 | Thiele – vr. 792 r. 767 to 742

In 2 Kings 15:2, we learn that Uzziah, also referred to as Azariah, reigned for 52 years in Jerusalem. Scholars suggest that the names Azariah and Uzziah are interchangeable, possibly being variant spellings of the same name. Uzziah, using his more commonly known name, was thrust into the spotlight at a very young age. His father, Amaziah, had unnecessarily provoked a significant conflict with Jehoash of Israel. After his army suffered defeat, the Israelites ransacked Jerusalem, demolished 600 feet of the city wall, and took hostages, including King Amaziah himself. He was likely kept in captivity before eventually being released to reign over the remnants of a once-great kingdom.

Upon Amaziah's return from Israel, he found himself in a precarious position, as a king on the run from conspirators within his kingdom who blamed him for the damage he had caused. When a king's life was in danger from external threats or failing health, he often appointed his eldest son to act as coregent. Uzziah was crowned as coregent at the age of five to ensure that there would be no dispute over the rightful heir after his father's death. After years of evading various assassins, Amaziah was executed in Lachish when Uzziah was just sixteen years old.

The accepted calculation has serious flaws:

Thiele's perspective suggests that Amaziah and Uzziah were coregents for 24 years, which is difficult to accept. First, it is necessary to address the clear statement in 2 Kings 14:19-21:

"And they made a conspiracy against him in Jerusalem, and he fled to Lachish. But they sent after him to Lachish and put him to death there. And they brought him on horses, and he was buried in Jerusalem with his fathers in the city of David. And all the people of Judah took Azariah, who was sixteen years old, and made him king instead of his father Amaziah." (ESV)

At this point, Thiele introduces the idea of a 24-year coregency with Amaziah. If Uzziah was sixteen when Amaziah died, how could he have been appointed coregent eight years before he was born?

According to Thiele, McFall, and others, the text of 2 Kings 15:1 is deemed incorrect and should instead read "in the 3rd year of Jeroboam" rather than "in the 27th year." By changing the date to fit his proposed timeline and asserting that Uzziah served as viceroy for 24 years, Thiele manipulated the subsequent figures regarding Uzziah's reign, effectively violating cross-references until the end of the Divided Kingdom in 722 BCE. Thiele did not originate this idea; it traces back to the 1909 *International Standard Bible Encyclopaedia* (ISBE), which also proposed the viceroy relationship that Uzziah had with his father during the same 24 years that Thiele later adopted.

Thiele's hypothesis becomes even more non-compliant with the Scriptures:

The appointment of Uzziah as coregent in 800 BCE marks the reference point from which the reigns of five Israelite kings are measured, the final one being Pekah. When constructing the timeline, it became challenging to determine the date of Uzziah's coregency by following a chronological order. Therefore, it was necessary to establish the later dates in the timeline to work backward to the common starting points for the reigns of Zechariah, Shallum, Menahem, Pekahiah, and Pekah.

According to Thiele, Uzziah's coregency (which Thiele refers to as a viceroyship) with Amaziah began in 792 BCE, and his sole reign was from 767 to 742 BCE after his father's death. Based on these figures, Uzziah reigned for 50 years rather than 52.

Serious doubts about the Thiele hypothesis:

According to the calculations presented in this book, the coregency between Amaziah and Uzziah lasted for eleven years. The unsupported claim of a 24-year coregency introduces an error of 13 years. In line with sound accounting practices, any error in the accounts must eventually resurface. E.R. Thiele accounted for the non-accession system in his analysis, absorbing one of the 13 years and leaving a balance of 12 years to consider at the end of the reigns of the kings of Israel.

The pivotal moment occurred during the kingship of Pekah. As stated in 2 Kings 15:27:

"Pekah son of Remaliah began to rule over Israel in the fifty-second year of King Uzziah's reign in Judah. He reigned in Samaria for twenty years." (NLT)

According to Thiele's calculations, Pekah began to reign in 752 BCE. This date is

40 years after his calculation for the beginning of Uzziah's reign, which is 12 years short of the stated fifty-second year.

Rather than acknowledge the flaws in his timeline, Thiele argued that the compilers of the biblical texts had made an error. To rectify this, he took the unusual step of changing the order of the reigns listed in 2 Kings 17 and 18 to fit his mathematical model, an action that no responsible historian or biblical scholar would typically undertake.

This book asserts a date of 952 BCE for the beginning of the Divided Kingdom, while Thiele's calculation concludes at 931 BCE. The 21-year error introduced by Thiele stems from his misinterpretation of several vital biblical and historical synchronisms.

Edwin Thiele deliberately compressed the Hebrew timeline to align with the Assyrian timeline, particularly beginning with the reigns of Ahab and Jehu. If this were merely an accusation, it would likely be denied vigorously. However, Thiele's work, as he admitted, was structured to fit the Assyrian timeline, which, unbeknownst to him, had also been compressed due to the omission of a 21-year reign, specifically that of Shammu-ramat (830/29 – 809/08).

The reign of Uzziah

During the first part of Uzziah's reign, he achieved significant military and domestic successes. One of his initial actions was to rebuild the town of Elath and restore it to Judean control. This port city, situated at the northern end of the Gulf of Aqaba, was a crucial hub for trade. Militarily, Uzziah fortified many cities and installed machines designed to hurl large stones, marking the first historical reference to catapults.

According to 2 Chronicles 26, Uzziah conquered the Philistines and the Arabians, and he received tribute from the Ammonites. He expanded the kingdom to cover as much territory as Judah had controlled since the days of Jehoshaphat.

However, Uzziah's successes led to arrogance. He entered the Temple of the Lord to burn incense on the altar of incense (2 Chronicles 26:16 NLT). Uzziah, confronted by eighty priests, became afflicted with leprosy on his forehead and had to leave the Temple. The term for leprosy used here, *tzaraath*, can refer to various skin conditions that rendered a person ritually impure.

Uzziah, the son of Amaziah, began to rule over Judah in the twenty-seventh year of King Jeroboam II's reign in Israel (2 Kings 15:1 NLT). Although he was crowned king at the age of sixteen following his father's death, Uzziah was twenty-eight during the twenty-seventh year of Jeroboam's reign. This passage signals a change in the status of his reign, for he ruled in a limited capacity due to his condition as a leper, living in seclusion in a house adjacent to the palace.

When Jotham was about twelve, he became the Governor of the Palace to transmit the wishes of Uzziah, who was forced to reign in quarantine. It appears that Uzziah sought to remain recognized as the sole ruler of the land, but Jotham eventually emerged as the public face of the kingdom. By the age of twenty-five, Jotham became vice-regent, which obliged his countrymen to address him as king. Consequently, King Jotham and King Jeroboam II of Israel reigned concurrently for approximately two years.

Uzziah spent the remainder of his days in quarantine, reigning with Jotham as his proxy. As his health deteriorated, he promoted Jotham to co-regent in 750 BCE, before abdicating in 749 BCE, just prior to his death in 748 BCE.

Zechariah of Israel (762n – 762t)
For reference: Ussher's dates – 773 to 772 | Thiele's date – 753

The reign of Zechariah, son of Jeroboam, as described in 2 Kings 15:8-10, lasted only six months. Some scholars, following the chronology of James Ussher, suggest that he may have ruled for an additional twelve years, but there is no historical evidence to support this claim. Readers will notice a recurring theme in which both Ushher and Thiele attempt to fit the figure of twelve years into various gaps that appear promising.

There is no record of Jeroboam II promoting Zechariah to a vice-regency, and such instances are rarely acknowledged unless there is some extraordinary circumstance that brings them to light.

It is important to note that biblical records consistently show reigns lasting less than a full year following a coronation as the actual term of the reign, not rounded up to a full year. While Zechariah may have had some influence during the transitional period following Jeroboam II's death, this period is not considered an official reign. Only officially recognized reigns are included in the list of Israelite kings.

Shallum of Israel (761n for 1 month)

For reference: Ussher's date – 772 | Thiele's date – 752

Shallum conspired against Zechariah and assassinated him in public, subsequently becoming the next king. *"Shallum son of Jabesh began to rule over Israel in the thirty-ninth year of King Uzziah's reign in Judah"* (2 Kings 15:13). Zechariah, his predecessor, was crowned in Nisan. As the next coronation date was six months later, Shallum reigned for that duration during his Zero Year.

Shallum's brief reign is significant for understanding the regional timeline, as it confirms the practice of accession-year accounting. Zechariah began his rule in Nisan during Uzziah's thirty-eighth year. Shallum ascended the throne in Tishri of the same year after killing his predecessor. His reign as king officially began after the New Year celebrations that followed his coronation.

According to the accession-year system, the New Year following a king's death marks the start of the new king's reign. Therefore, Shallum's effective reign lasted for seven months: six months of his Zero Year reign and one month following his formal coronation.

Menahem of Israel (Iyar 761 – 751 Adar)

For reference: Ussher's dates – 772 to 761 | Thiele's dates – 752 to 742

Because Shallum survived only the first month of his reign, Menahem had the opportunity to be crowned immediately, instead of having to wait until the following year. According to 2 Kings 15:13 and 2 Kings 15:17, Uzziah's thirty-ninth year marks the beginning of the reigns of both Shallum and Menahem, which supports the idea of accession-year accounting.

Menahem was a ruthless leader. He murdered everyone in the town of Tiphsah and the surrounding countryside after they refused to accept him. As a horrific example, he tore apart pregnant women. Besides the later invasion by the Assyrians, the biblical accounts reveal little about Menahem, as noted in 2 Kings 15:21: *"And the rest of the acts of Menahem, and all that he did, are they not written in the book of the chronicles of the kings of Israel?"* Accessing those chronicles would be helpful, but that book was lost long ago.

Pul was the same as Tiglath-pileser

There are two conflicting versions of the order of reigns for the latter kings of Israel. One version appears in 2 Kings 17 and 18, while the other comes from the reorganization performed by Edwin Thiele. Thiele struggled to align the biblical timeline with the Assyrian model. He suggested that the scribes had made errors and recorded the reigns in the wrong order. To resolve this issue, he adjusted the timing of the reigns to fit his hypothesis. One of his key assertions was that Pul and Tiglath-pileser were the same person.

Throughout this study, the central assumption has been that the biblical data is correct. It is difficult to establish an absolute set of synchronisms without first creating a foundation of conservative assumptions that is essential for achieving perfect harmony.

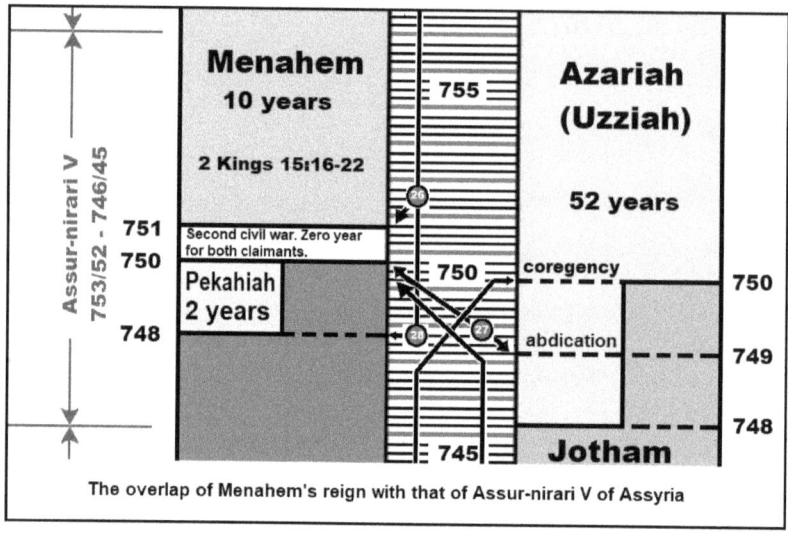

The overlap of Menahem's reign with that of Assur-nirari V of Assyria

By examining the timeline of each reign and cross-referencing the information, we can gain a clearer understanding of the interactions that took place. If we accept the biblical record as accurate, we find that Menahem's reign ended approximately six years before Tiglath Pileser began his rule over Assyria in 745/44 BCE. Assur Nirari V was the ruler when Assyria invaded Israel during Menahem's leadership.

"And Pul, the king of Assyria, came against the land. Menahem gave Pul a thousand talents of silver (about 37 tons) so that his support would help confirm Menahem's kingdom." (2 Kings 15:19, KJV). In the New Living Translation (NLT), the name "Pul" is replaced with "Tiglath Pileser" in 2 Kings 15:19. A footnote explains that Pul is another name for Tiglath Pileser.

Although the chart accompanying this study appears to eliminate any possibility of overlap between the reigns of Menahem and Tiglath Pileser, an Assyrian inscription requires consideration. This inscription is likely the reason Thiele rearranged the order of these reigns. Known as *The Annals of Tiglath Pileser* (ANET3 283), it includes a fragment stating: *"I received tribute from Kuštašpi of Commagene,*

Rezon of Damascus, Menahem of Samaria...". The inscription goes on to list several other regional leaders.

A coregency between Assur Nirai V and Tiglath Pileser III

The biblical timeline supporting the comprehensive chart aligns precisely with existing data. Tiglath Pileser III interacted with Menahem during the reign of Assur Nirari V, and the Hebrew scriptures refer to him as "King." This title strongly suggests that these two monarchs served as coregents for much of Assur Nirari V's reign. Although Assyrian records do not explicitly state this coregency, historians must reconcile various biblical events to gain a better understanding of it.

Some historians suggest a brief period of co-rule due to chronological discrepancies. However, given that Menahem died six years before Tiglath Pileser's reign, the proposed "brief period" may have been quite significant.

The background of that period involved the unprecedented transfer of power from the throne to local governors, who acted more like independent city-states than as part of a centralised kingdom. During this time, several officials produced stelae extolling their achievements, making no mention of the king. Assur Nirari V was a weak and ineffective ruler. At the same time, Tiglath Pileser III, believed to be either his son or brother, aimed to restore centralised power to the throne he would eventually inherit.

A likely scenario is that Tiglath Pileser was appointed as coregent and began the process of centralisation. He conducted military campaigns and erected stelae in his honour. After a few years of military successes, his rising prominence in Assyria posed a threat to his brother's authority, leading to civil conflict just before Assur Nirari V's death. Tiglath Pileser ultimately usurped the throne.

Thiele recognised the probability of a coregency but chose to rearrange the order of the Israelite kings instead of incorporating the possibility of a coregency into the

Assyrian timeline. At the time of the publication of *MNHK* in 1951, the prevailing opinion was that there were no coregencies in the Assyrian chronology.

The timelines of the Hebrew and Assyrian records regarding Menahem's reign can coexist without disrupting either set of synchronisms. Historian Edwin Thiele proposed a controversial twelve-year period during which Menahem and his son Pekahiah supposedly shared control of the Kingdom of Israel alongside King Pekah. According to Thiele, they governed separate territories: Pekah ruled in Gilead, while Menahem and Pekahiah were in charge of Samaria (Thiele, 1986:63).

Thiele aimed to align events described in *The Annals of Tiglath Pileser*, which occurred before his sole reign began in 745/44 BCE, with recorded events that took place in 738 BCE during his official reign.

The Second Civil War in Israel – 751/750 BCE: An Analysis

The death of Menahem sparked a power struggle in Israel. Pekah, a general in the army, saw this as a chance to challenge Pekahiah, Menahem's son. Menahem had been known for his harsh rule, and his death created unrest that weakened his son's position. This action led to a civil conflict that lasted approximately a year, although some believe it could have been as short as a few months.

A key aspect of this conflict is that Pekahiah was not crowned during the New Year celebrations, indicating another claim to the throne. He began his rule upon his father's death but operated as an uncrowned leader for over a year.

Support for a gap year appears in the following two verses:

"Menahem son of Gadi began to rule over Israel in the thirty-ninth year of King Uzziah's reign in Judah. He reigned in Samaria ten years." (2 Kings 15:17, NLT)

"Pekahiah son of Menahem began to rule over Israel in the fiftieth year of King Uzziah's reign in Judah. He reigned in Samaria two years." (2 Kings 15:23, NLT)

Although Menahem reigned for ten years, Pekahiah's official reign began eleven years after his father began to reign. The one-year discrepancy resulted in a delay of Pekahiah's coronation due to civil conflict.

The conflict ended with both sides dividing Israel and ruling different territories, possibly to protect against outside threats. Two years later, after assassinating Pekahiah, Pekah seized control and unified the divided nation.

Pekahiah faced significant delays in ascending to power, indicating challenges to his succession. Historical records from Tiglath Pileser III, as noted by scholar Stanley Rosenbaum, confirm the existence of two separate kingdoms in northern Israel during this period. Other scholars, including H. J. Cook and Carl Lederer, suggest that Pekah established a rival reign in Gilead, opposing Menahem's rule in Samaria.

The writings of the prophet Hosea, who is believed to have lived during the eighth century BCE and died around 725 BCE, further support the existence of these concurrent kingdoms. Hosea's text provides a vivid narrative that reflects the political and spiritual crises of the time:

"Hear these things, ye priests; and attend, O house of Israel; and hearken, O house of the king; for the controversy is with you, because ye have been a snare in Scopia [Mizpah], and as a net spread on Itabyrium [Tabor], which those who hunt prey have fixed: but I will correct you. I know Ephraim, and Israel is not far from me; for now, Ephraim has gone grievously astray; Israel is defiled ... And the pride of Israel shall be brought low before his face; and Israel and Ephraim shall fall in their iniquities; and Judah also shall fall with them" (Hosea 5:1–3, 5 LXX).

These verses, sourced from the Septuagint, highlight the clear thematic distinction among three separate polities: Ephraim, Israel, and Judah.

Pekahiah of Israel (750n – 748 Adar)

For reference: Ussher's dates – 761 to 759; Thiele's dates – 742 to 740

In the fiftieth year of Azariah's reign over Judah, Pekahiah, the son of Menahem, ascended the throne in Samaria and ruled for two years (2 Kings 15:23). This year also marked the beginning of Pekahiah's rule, coinciding with Pekah's rise to power in the northern territories of Israel, particularly those governed from Gilead. The authors of the Books of Kings found it challenging to present these reigns clearly to readers.

As Menahem's designated heir, Pekahiah's short reign required adherence to traditional reporting methods. The year following Menahem's death did not see a coronation due to a civil uprising led by Pekah. Pekahiah and Pekah ruled over different portions of Israel after they reached a compromise. This arrangement lasted for two years.

After Pekah assassinated Pekahiah, he took control and governed the previously divided regions, establishing himself as the undisputed monarch. His reign then extended over twenty years, encompassing both his time in Gilead and the years of unified rule.

Pekah of Israel (750n – 730 Elul)

For reference: Ussher's dates – 759 to 739; Thiele's dates – 752 to 732

In the fifty-second year of King Azariah of Judah, Pekah, the son of Remaliah, became king of Israel in Samaria, ruling for twenty years (2 Kings 15:27). Pekah's reign began in 750 BCE, which aligns with the start of Pekahiah's rule.

This study notes that Pekah, like other kings of Israel and Judah, is said to have "begun to reign" from the date he started ruling over the entire nation of Israel, not just a portion of it. However, his reign's length includes the two years he ruled over half of the country from Gilead.

There is a significant connection between Pekah's rule and Jotham's reign: *"In the second year of Pekah, Jotham began to reign"* (2 Kings 15:32). If Pekah began his twenty-year reign in Uzziah's fiftieth year, then his second year would occur just before Uzziah's death. Conversely, if we adopt a stricter interpretation that Pekah's reign began in Uzziah's fifty-second year, Jotham would start his reign a year after Uzziah's death, resulting in an unsupported gap in the timeline.

Therefore, it is evident that Pekah's reign started in 750 BCE. Additionally, as noted in 2 Kings 17:2, *"In the seventeenth year of Pekah, Ahaz began to reign,"* which indicates that Ahaz ascended to the throne in 732 BCE. By tracing back Pekah's reign from 750n BCE, we can confirm that Jotham reigned for sixteen years, suggesting he was appointed co-regent in 750t BCE, a year before Uzziah stepped down. Confirming this complex timeline may require regular consultation of the chronological chart and careful analysis of Uzziah's reign.

The difficulties in aligning the synchronisms during this period have led many scholars to question the reliability of the biblical accounts regarding Pekah. This study centres on the assumption that we can reconcile the biblical data, and the approach taken finds no contradiction of either Assyrian or Hebrew synchronisms during Pekah's reign.

John Ferris

CHAPTER 8

Jotham of Judah (750t – 734 Elul)

For reference: Ussher – vr. 768; r. 759 to 742; Thiele – vr. 750; r. 740 to 732

Jotham became king at the age of twenty-five and ruled for sixteen years in Jerusalem, as noted in 2 Chronicles 27:1. However, this seemingly simple statement masks the complexities of Jotham's life story.

He grew up in the palace as the son of Uzziah, one of the mightiest kings in the history of Judah. When Jotham was around twelve, his father contracted leprosy and had to live in seclusion in a separate house next to the palace. Rather than appointing Jotham as vice regent, which would have granted him the title of "King Jotham," Uzziah designated him as "Governor of the Palace." In this role, Jotham acted as Uzziah's proxy, and it appears that Uzziah wanted to be the only person in the land referred to as king. As time passed, Jotham began to judge the land and became the public figurehead of the Kingdom of Judah.

At the age of twenty-five, Jotham was finally appointed as vice regent, at which point he became known as King Jotham. The coronation occurred around 764 BCE, approximately two years before the death of Jeroboam II of Israel. King Jotham and King Jeroboam reigned concurrently, as evidenced by 1 Chronicles 5:17, which states, *"All of these were listed in the genealogical records during the days of King Jotham of Judah and King Jeroboam of Israel."*

The timelines of Ussher and Thiele contradict the idea that these two kings ruled simultaneously.

As Uzziah neared the end of his life, he appointed Jotham as coregent. This appointment took place in 750 BCE, as confirmed by 2 Kings 15:30: *"Then Hoshea began to rule over Israel in the twentieth year of King Jotham, son of Uzziah."* The date of Hoshea's accession occurred in Nisan 730 BCE. Counting back to the beginning of Jotham's reign brings us to Tishri 750 BCE, which is two years before Uzziah's death.

Within a year, Uzziah abdicated the throne. Although the text does not state it explicitly, Jotham took over and "began to reign," a phrase commonly used to signal a change of status. In 2 Kings 15:32 it states, *"Jotham son of Uzziah began to rule over Judah in the second year of King Pekah's reign in Israel."*

The progression of Jotham's status was from Governor of the Palace (777 BCE), to Vice Regent (764 BCE), to coregent (750 BCE), ultimately exercising the power of a sole king upon his father's abdication in 749 BCE. Uzziah died the following year, in 748 BCE, marking the end of his fifty two year reign.

In 742 BCE, Jotham appointed his son Ahaz as coregent, and they ruled together until 734 BCE when Ahaz deposed his father. According to 2 Kings 16:1, Ahaz began to rule in the seventeenth year of Pekah's reign. Although Jotham was deposed, he survived and lived for at least another four years. Scholars record his official reign as lasting sixteen years.

When cross referencing with Hoshea's reign, the text specifies it as Jotham's twentieth year. This instance suggests that as long as he lived, scribes could use the beginning of his reign as a reference point. Though his official reign lasted sixteen years, he had been exercising power for approximately forty three years before being deposed.

During the latter part of his reign, both Israel and Syria, along with a resurgent Assyria, posed significant threats to Judah. It seems that Ahaz aligned himself with a pro Assyria faction, which forced Jotham into an unwilling retirement.

Ahaz of Judah (742t – 726 Elul)

For reference: Ussher's dates – 742 to 726; Thiele – vr. 735; r. 732 to 715

"Ahaz was twenty years old when he became king, and he reigned in Jerusalem for sixteen years." (2 Kings 16:2 NLT) A casual reader might assume that Ahaz died at the age of thirty six. However, his son Hezekiah is recorded as being twenty five when he began to reign. This discrepancy suggests that there is more to the story than meets the eye.

His father Jotham is noted to have begun his reign at the age of twenty five, which indicates that he might have been appointed as king when he was made vice regent. Similarly, Jotham likely appointed Ahaz as vice regent after the death of Uzziah. This appointment would have taken place around six years before Ahaz's official elevation to coregent, indicated by 742 BCE.

Ahaz's age at death was approximately forty two, and it is much more plausible that he became a father at seventeen rather than at eleven. The scholar Ussher quoted Immanuel Tremellius (1510–1580), who had arrived at a similar conclusion.

Shortly after Ahaz deposed his father in 734 BCE, Israel under Pekah and the Arameans under Rezin joined forces to attack Jerusalem. During this conflict, enemy forces killed 120,000 Judean soldiers and captured 200,000 women and children, taking them to Samaria. The prophet Oded intervened, and the captives returned to Judah.

During the attack on Jerusalem, the Edomites capitalised on the distraction to recapture the seaport of Elath and drive out the Judeans. In desperation, Ahaz, ignoring the advice of the prophet Isaiah, sought assistance from Tiglath Pileser, the Assyrian king. He sent a letter with his request that stated, *"I am your servant and your vassal. Come up and rescue me from the attacking armies of Aram and Israel."* (2 Kings 16:7 NLT).

Tiglath Pileser did come, but instead of helping Ahaz, he attacked him. To appease the Assyrian king, Ahaz took gold and silver from the Temple, the palace, and the homes of officials, giving it all to Tiglath Pileser, whose attention then turned to the Israelites and the Arameans.

Between 734 and 732 BCE, Assyria defeated Aram, killed King Rezin, captured Damascus, and led the population away as captives. Similarly, northern Israel was captured as far south as Jezreel, encompassing Gilead and Galilee, including all the land of Naphtali, with the people deported to Assyria.

After Ahaz had been relieved of his enemies, he became obsessed with the pagan religion of the Assyrians and adopted many of their practices. *"He even offered sacrifices in the valley of Ben Hinnom, including sacrificing his own sons in the fire."* (2 Chronicles 28:3). Great cruelty marked his reign, and he was not held in high regard by his people.

When Ahaz died, he was buried in Jerusalem. His name "Ahaz" is a shortened form of "Jehoahaz," which means "Yahweh has held." Due to his nefarious actions, the first part of his name referring to the God of the Hebrews was omitted.

At about the age of forty, Ahaz was ruling Israel during a time of peace, with no immediate threats from enemies. Although Scripture does not provide details about Ahaz's death, it can be inferred that he appointed his son Hezekiah as coregent two years before his passing. This move suggests there may have been a sudden decline in Ahaz's health around 728 BCE, leading him to share power with his son.

Hoshea of Israel (730n – Elul 722)

For reference: Ussher's dates – 730 to 721; Thiele's dates – 732 to 722

In the twelfth year of Ahaz, king of Judah, Hoshea, the son of Elah, ascended to the throne of Israel in Samaria, where he ruled for nine years (2 Kings 17:1).

Hoshea had been a captain in King Pekah's army and held a pro Assyrian stance. He assassinated Pekah, and as a reward, Tiglath Pileser appointed him as king over

Israel. An Assyrian inscription describes this event, noting: *"Israel (literally: 'Omri house' or 'Bit Humria') overthrew their king Pekah (Pa qa ha) and I placed Hoshea (A ú si') as king over them. I received from them ten talents of gold and one thousand talents of silver as their tribute and brought them to Assyria."*

Once installed as king, Hoshea remained loyal to Tiglath Pileser. However, when Shalmaneser V came to power, Hoshea grew frustrated with the heavy tribute demanded by Assyria and eventually defaulted on it. He entered negotiations with Pharaoh So (also known as Osorkon IV, reigning from 730 to 716) of Egypt (2 Kings 17:4) in an attempt to free himself from Assyrian control. When news of this treason reached Shalmaneser, he had Hoshea arrested and imprisoned. Shalmaneser then proceeded to besiege Samaria for three years before the Israelites capitulated and the city fell.

When did the siege of Samaria begin?

In 2 Kings 18:9, it states, "And it came to pass in the fourth year of King Hezekiah, which was the seventh year of Hoshea son of Elah, king of Israel, that Shalmaneser king of Assyria came up against Samaria and besieged it" (NLT). This conflict began in the fourth year of Hezekiah, which spans from 1 Tishri 725 to 29 Elul 724. The seventh year of Hoshea is from 1 Nisan 724 to 29 Adar 723. There is a six month overlap for the potential dates for when the siege began, specifically from 1 Nisan 724 to 29 Elul 724.

When did the siege of Samaria end?

2 Kings 18:10 states, "And at the end of three years they took it: even in the sixth year of Hezekiah, that is, in the ninth year of Hoshea king of Israel, Samaria was taken." The sixth year of Hezekiah spans from 1 Tishri 723 to 29 Elul 722, while the ninth year of Hoshea is from 1 Nisan 722 to 29 Adar 721. The overlapping period of these dates runs from 1 Nisan 722 to 29 Elul 722.

The available date range indicates a period of one and a half years (from 29 Elul 724 to 1 Nisan 722) to two and a half years (from 1 Nisan 724 to 29 Elul 722). Since 2 Kings 18:10 specifies three years, the latter range aligns with the narrative.

It was Shalmaneser V, not Sargon II, who initially captured Samaria, despite Sargon II's later claims at the end of his reign that he was the conqueror. The date for the defeat of Samaria appears to be around September 722 BCE.

Events after the defeat of Samaria

"In the ninth year of Hoshea the king of Assyria took Samaria, and carried Israel away into Assyria, and placed them in Halah and in Habor by the river of Gozan, and in the cities of the Medes." (2 Kings 17:9 KJV)

Sennacherib's siege of Lachish during the reign of Hezekiah

Most of the population of Samaria were resettled and absorbed into cities of Assyria and Media, and Shalmaneser repopulated the territory with citizens from Assyria. "And the king of Assyria brought men from Babylon, and from Cuthah, and from Ava, and from Hamath, and from Sepharvaim, and placed them in the cities of Samaria instead of the children of Israel: and they possessed Samaria, and dwelt in the cities thereof." (2 Kings 17:24 KJV)

Hezekiah of Judah (728t – 699 Elul)

For reference: Ussher – vr. 726 r. 726 to 698. Thiele – vr. 729 r. 716/15 to 687/86.

This plaque is displayed inside Hezekiah Tunnel

Hezekiah began his reign at the age of twenty five and ruled for twenty nine years in Jerusalem, as documented in 2 Kings 18:2. Notably, he was appointed as coregent two years before his father Ahaz's death. It is likely that he turned twenty five in the year of Ahaz's death, and that Hezekiah died at the age of fifty two.

A note to readers in relation to the Assyrian record

This study concludes at the end of the period of the Divided Kingdom, following the fall of Samaria in 722 BCE. After this point, there can be no further cross references between the two kingdoms. The timeline has been established independently, without relying on Assyrian dates to support the interpretation of the Hebrew numbers.

These calculations primarily depend on the assumption that the biblical data accurately represent historical records. When the biblical account mentions interactions with Assyria and presents contradictions or paradoxes, we assume that the biblical account holds precedence. Once we complete this analysis, we can use the biblical timeline to correct errors or false assumptions in the Assyrian timeline.

Thiele mirrors this process by assuming the Assyrian record is infallible and uses it as a template to measure the Hebrew record. The reign of Hezekiah represents a critical point in history that has been marred by a series of misinterpretations related to the reigns of Sargon II and Sennacherib. A later section will focus on the evidence that supports the view that Sargon II and Sennacherib served as coregents from the start of Sargon's reign until he died in 705 BCE.

The Siege of Jerusalem in 715/714 BCE

The biblical record is clear. According to 2 Kings 18:13, "In the fourteenth year of King Hezekiah, Sennacherib, king of Assyria, came up against all the fortified cities of Judah and captured them." Hezekiah began his reign in Tishri 728 BCE, which means that his fourteenth year would be 715/714 BCE.

The consensus about the 701 BCE date

Academics generally agree that Sennacherib besieged Jerusalem in 701 BCE, based on the interpretation of "prisms," which are nearly identical hexagonal artifacts revealing details of eight military campaigns waged by Sennacherib. Given that his father died in 705 BCE, it is reasonable to assume that the record pertains to events that occurred after that date. Thiele concluded that Sennacherib's Third Campaign, which targeted Jerusalem, took place in 701 BCE.

However, an analysis of the eight campaigns indicates that seven of them reconstruct the events of Sargon II's campaigns. They are listed in the same chronological order and involve the exact locations, events, and figures. We propose that Sargon and Sennacherib were coregents from the start of Sargon's reign. Evidence supporting this proposition will be discussed later in this study in the section dedicated to Sennacherib.

The consequences of Thiele's hypothesis

By assigning 701 BCE as the date for the siege of Jerusalem, Thiele has had to adjust the reigns of Jotham, Ahaz, Hezekiah, and Manasseh to fit his timeline. Since the blockade occurred during Hezekiah's fourteenth year, historians assign Hezekiah's reign to 715 BCE.

This adjustment also implies that Ahaz was alive until 716 rather than 726. Because Hezekiah began to reign in the third year of Hoshea (2 Kings 18:1), Thiele assumes a vice regency for Hezekiah with Ahaz starting in 729. Due to the errors carried through the accounting of reigns, he has also proposed a ten year coregency between Hezekiah and Manasseh.

Thiele's methodology often involves manipulating data to fit his narrative. For instance, he stated, "To my surprise and dismay, the fourteenth year of Hezekiah turned out to be 702 instead of 701…. The last year of Hoshea and the fall of Samaria was 711" (Thiele, 1983, p. 17). Initially, Thiele calculated the fall of Samaria to be in 711 BCE; however, he later revised this to 722 BCE to align with the prevailing consensus among Assyriologists. Revisions aimed at meeting the expectations of fellow Assyriologists raise concerns about the credibility of Thiele's work.

Summary of the life of Hezekiah

Hezekiah was born in 751 BCE, just a few years before his great grandfather Uzziah passed away. His grandfather Jotham reigned until Hezekiah was seventeen, at which point his father Ahaz deposed Jotham and began his own reign. Hezekiah witnessed the good that prevailed during his grandfather's rule, but he also observed the evil embraced by his father, which included the horrific practice of making

Hezekiah "pass through the fire" (2 Kings 16:3), a ritual that usually resulted in death.

Having experienced his father's devotion to the Assyrian cause, as well as his obsession with Assyrian gods, it is not surprising that Hezekiah chose a different path when he ascended the throne after his father's demise.

Not only did he refuse to pay tribute to Assyria, but he also destroyed all the pagan symbols in the land, as described in 2 Kings 18:4–7: "He removed the pagan shrines, smashed the sacred pillars, and cut down the Asherah poles. He broke up the bronze serpent that Moses had made, because the people of Israel had been offering sacrifices to it. The bronze serpent was called Nehushtan."

"Hezekiah trusted in the Lord, the God of Israel. There was no one like him among all the kings of Judah, either before or after his time. He remained faithful to the Lord in everything and carefully obeyed all the commands that the Lord had given to Moses. Consequently, the Lord was with him, and Hezekiah was successful in everything he did. He revolted against the king of Assyria and refused to pay him tribute."

After Shalmaneser V captured Samaria, he replaced the local population with his countrymen. Following this, an uprising led by his son, Sargon II, ensued. Shalmaneser either died or was exiled. Sargon, along with his coregent Sennacherib, launched multiple military campaigns beginning in 721 BCE. In 715/714 BCE, they advanced against Judah, conquering many cities and towns before besieging Jerusalem. Remarkably, the Scriptures attribute the death of 185,000 Assyrian soldiers overnight to "the angel of the Lord," which spared Jerusalem from destruction.

The historian Herodotus speculates that before invading Judah, the Assyrians faced Egypt and returned with prisoners who were infected with a plague, possibly spread by mice. This event may represent the earliest recorded instance of the Bubonic Plague.

During this time, King Hezekiah also fell ill but was miraculously restored to health. However, he had not married. According to Jewish tradition, the prophet Isaiah encouraged him to marry and have an heir. About fifteen years before his death, Hezekiah married Isaiah's daughter, Hephzibah. When Hezekiah died in 699 BCE, his son Manasseh was just twelve years old.

From Manasseh to the last king of Judah, Zedekiah

During Hezekiah's reign, Samaria ceased to exist, and Judah would last just over a century before being defeated by Babylon and sent into exile. The remaining reigns do not have any recorded coregencies, although E. R. Thiele argues that there was a coregency between Hezekiah and Manasseh. The calculations moving forward are linear and adhere to the rules of accession. Brief explanations of these reigns will follow.

Manasseh of Judah (699t – 644 Elul)

For reference: Ussher's dates – 698 to 643. Thiele – vr. 697 r. 686 to 642.

The biblical account in 2 Kings 21:1 notes, "Manasseh was twelve years old when he began to reign and reigned fifty five years in Jerusalem." Manasseh's reign was the longest of any in the histories of Israel or Judah. He reversed all the religious changes made by his father and reintroduced polytheistic practices. Judah succumbed to the Assyrians under his watch, and Manasseh became a faithful vassal. "Manasseh also murdered many innocent people until Jerusalem was filled from one end to the other with innocent blood." (2 Kings 21:16 NLT)

He must have offended the Assyrians, "So the Lord sent the commanders of the Assyrian armies, and they took Manasseh prisoner. They put a ring through his nose, bound him in bronze chains, and led him away to Babylon." In his distress, he called out to God and repented. He was returned to Jerusalem, and he cleared Judah of all the pagan gods and altars, restoring worship of Yahweh. However, the damage had already been done.

Amon of Judah (644t – 642 Elul)

For reference: Ussher's dates – 643 to 641. Thiele's dates – 642 to 640.

Amon ascended to the throne at the age of twenty two and reigned for two years in Jerusalem, as documented in 2 Chronicles 33:21. Although the account of Amon's reign is brief, it is evident that he followed in his father's evil practices and did not embrace the repentance of his father. After two years in power, he was assassinated by his servants, who were later executed. Following this, the people installed Amon's eight year old son, Josiah, as the new king.

Josiah of Judah (642t – 611 Elul)

For reference: Ussher's dates – 640 to 609. Thiele's dates – 641 to 609.

King Josiah of Judah began his reign at the age of eight, as recorded in 2 Chronicles 34:1: "Josiah was eight years old when he began to reign, and he reigned in Jerusalem for thirty one years."

According to the Babylonian Chronicle, the battle at Harran—between the Assyrians and their Egyptian allies on one side, and the Babylonians on the other—occurred between the months of Tammuz (July to August) and Elul (August to September) in the year 609 BCE. Josiah met his demise during the month of Tammuz (July to August) of that year, as Egyptian forces advanced toward Harran.

To address chronological discrepancies, we must consider a one-year error in Ptolemy's Canon, as identified by Faulsich, and an addition year resulting from calculations describing the reigns of Jehoahaz of Judah and Jehoiakim. These considerations lead us to revise the date of Josiah's death to 611 BCE. This recalibration highlights the complexities of historical chronology during this period, ensuring the accuracy and reliability of our historical analysis.

Summary of the life of Josiah

Josiah was born in 650 BCE and became king at the age of eight. During his reign, he instituted significant religious reforms and eliminated the worship of foreign gods. Josiah came to power during a period of instability in the region. Assyria had become militarily weak, and Egypt had become a vassal state of Assyria. Meanwhile, Babylon was gaining strength, prompting Assyria to request military assistance from Egypt.

In the years leading up to the final battle in which Josiah died, Pharaoh Necho II ruled Egypt. At the same time, Judah broke free from Assyrian control and expanded its borders to include significant territories in Samaria that Assyria had controlled. Scholars suggest that Josiah was attempting to reestablish the Kingdom of David, but his ambitions led to the unwise decision to engage the Egyptian army in battle. Following his death, Judah entered a period of rapid decline.

Jehoahaz of Judah 611t – 611 Kislev

For reference: Ussher's dates – 609 to 609 | Thiele's dates – 609 to 609

The historical account of the early seventh century provides a detailed narrative regarding the death of King Josiah, who succumbed to his injuries in Jerusalem during the month of Tammuz, three months before the Judean New Year, which begins on 1 Tishri (September to October). After Josiah's death, his fourth son, Jehoahaz, was chosen as king, an event traditionally recorded as having occurred in 609 BCE. However, the scholarship presented in this book suggests that 611 BCE is the correct date.

This appointment took place after Necho's return from the battle at Harran and following the fatal confrontation with King Josiah at Megiddo. However, students of ancient history might dispute the 611 date. Earlier sections of this study present research that emphasises the need to recalibrate the datum point by one year, and incorporate another year to account for the circumstances surrounding the reigns of Jehoahaz and Jehoiakim for an accurate understanding of the events.

Jehoahaz, Josiah's immediate successor, reigned for three months following his coronation in the month of Tishri in 611. According to the biblical text, "Jehoahaz was twenty-three years old when he began to reign; he reigned three months in Jerusalem" (2 Kings 23:31). According to Hebrew succession rules, the three months between Josiah's death and Jehoahaz's coronation are considered his Zero Year. This calculation indicates that his total reign, including the Zero Year, lasted approximately six months. The reign of his successor, Jehoiakim, was counted from 1 Tishri in 610 BCE.

When Necho II returned from the unsuccessful siege of Harran, he discovered an unexpected turn of events: the Judeans had installed a new king without consulting him. He seized Jehoahaz and imprisoned him for the rest of his life, eventually replacing him with his older brother Eliakim, whom he renamed Jehoiakim.

There was a period of a few months before Necho II appointed Jehoiakim, during which the people of Judea were uncertain if Jehoahaz would be allowed to return to the throne. Under the Hebrew system, people regarded Jehoahaz as king, even while he remained imprisoned. There are several precedents for this situation. The Israelites imprisoned Amaziah, but he returned to his throne after his release. Hoshea remained the King of Israel even while the Assyrians imprisoned him three years before the fall of the kingdom. The Assyrians imprisoned Manasseh, but he resumed his role upon his release. Similarly, Jehoahaz was King of Judah for three months after his coronation, despite being detained for much of that time. When Necho II installed Jehoiakim on the throne, it marked the end of Jehoahaz's reign.

Jehoiakim of Judah (Tishri 610 – Elul 599)

For reference: Ussher's dates – 610 to 599 | Thiele's dates – 609 to 598

The cuneiform inscription on this clay tablet highlights the conquest of Jerusalem by Nebuchadnezzar II and the surrender of Jehoiakim, king of Judah

Jehoiakim ascended to the throne at the age of twenty-five and reigned for eleven years over the city of Jerusalem, as stated in 2 Kings 23:36. Pharaoh Necho II orchestrated his rise to kingship by removing his younger brother, Jehoahaz, after a brief three-month rule. Necho imprisoned Jehoahaz in Riblah, Syria, before relocating him to Egypt, where he spent the remainder of his life (2 Kings 23:34). Jehoiakim's reign is chronologically defined from Tishri in 610 BCE to no later than the end of Tishri in 599 BCE, the month marking the beginning of the Judean new year.

During this tumultuous period, the Hebrews adhered to the rules of accession. Necho II installed Jehoiakim as King of Judah in the month of Teveth in 611 BCE, the fourth month of the Judean year. Jehoiakim officially began his eleven-year reign in Tishri 610 BCE, although he had already been ruling for eight months during his Zero Year.

Jehoiakim ruled as a vassal of the Egyptians. However, after the Babylonians defeated the Egyptians at the Battle of Carchemish, Nebuchadnezzar II went on to besiege Jerusalem. To avoid destruction, Jehoiakim switched his allegiance and became a vassal to the Babylonians. He maintained this arrangement for three years until a failed invasion of Egypt weakened their control over the region, prompting Jehoiakim to revert to his allegiance with the Egyptians.

In late 599 BCE, Nebuchadnezzar II invaded Judah and laid siege to Jerusalem once again, a siege that lasted three months. Jehoiakim died before the siege concluded. Although he reigned for eleven years, he passed away before the end of the Tishri month in 599 BCE.

His reign was filled with murder, incest, and intrigue, and no one mourned his passing. Many contradictory accounts surround Jehoiakim's death.

The explanation for the one-year and two-year timeline discrepancies

The placement of this information is essential because the reigns of Jehoahaz and Jehoiakim centre around poorly understood circumstances, leading to a missing year in most other timelines produced. Instead of repeating all the details, readers should refer to the sections dedicated to those two kings.

In summary, Jehoahaz's reign lasted until the third month of the regnal year 611/610 BCE. His successor, Jehoiakim, was not formally crowned until the month of Tishri in 610 BCE. Other chronologists have condensed this information into a shorter timeframe, resulting in an error of one year. As a consequence, biblical events that occurred before the end of Jehoiakim's reign in 599 BCE are recorded as happening two years later.

This two-year discrepancy must account for the one-year error identified by

Faulsich. For instance, the Battle of Harran took place in 611 BCE, not 609. After Jehoiakim's reign, a calculation error of one year occurs, as only Faulsich's identified one-year error remains relevant.

The calculations that reveal these errors are based solely on the fully reconciled Hebrew record, although it is also essential to consider synchronisms with Babylonian and Assyrian records. As we examine Assyrian chronology, we will observe that margins of error become larger as we delve further back into the history of the Neo-Assyrian Empire. This empire began around the beginning of the Divided Kingdom and ended just before the Babylonians exiled the Jews.

The following section on Jehoiachin explains the underlying one-year error associated with Jehoiachin's reign.

Jehoiachin of Judah (21 Heshvan 599 to 2 Adar 598)

For reference: Ussher – vr. 609? -r. 599 to 599 | Thiele – vr. 607? -r. 598 to 597

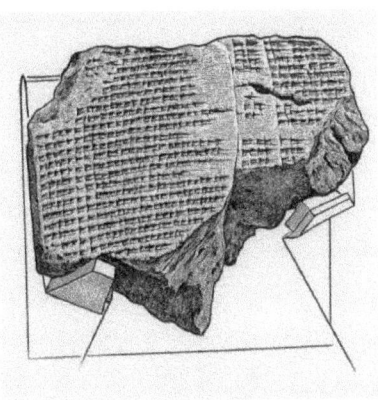

Clay tablet. The Akkadian cuneiform inscription lists certain rations and mentions the name of Jeconiah (Jehoiachin), King of Judah, and the Babylonian captivity.

King Jehoiachin, also known as Jeconiah, ascended to the throne at the age of eighteen, ruling over Jerusalem for a brief duration of three months (2 Kings 24:8) as a vassal of Babylonia. His reign commenced approximately three months and

137

ten days before 2 Adar 599, thereby positioning the conclusion of Jehoiachin's rule within the timeframe of 18 November 599 to 25 February 598.

Speculation suggests that Jehoiachin served as vice-regent for a decade before his elevation to kingship, having received this appointment in 609 BCE. According to the rules of succession, it could only have been a vice-regency.

The reign of Jehoiachin/Jeconiah serves as a critical anchor point within many historical chronologies and has been traditionally dated from 21 Heshvan 598 to 2 Adar 597 BCE. However, Faulsich has identified a one-year error in the application of Ptolemy's eclipse information to the historical record. All dates that use Jehoiachin's surrender as a datum point are one year in arrears. The corrected dates are 21 Heshvan 599 to 2 Adar 598 BCE.

The Babylonian Chronicle Number 5 provides details of Jehoiachin's capture: "The seventh year [of Nebuchadrezzar]: In the month of Kislev the king of Akkad mustered his army and marched to Hattu. He encamped against the city of Judah (i.e., Jerusalem) and on the second day of the month of Adar, he captured the city and seized the king. A king of his own choice he appointed in the city and taking the vast tribute, he brought it into Babylon."

Zedekiah of Judah (598t – Tammuz 587)

For reference: Ussher's dates – 599 to 588 | Thiele's dates – 597 to 586

Zedekiah was appointed to the throne by the Babylonian King Nebuchadnezzar at the age of twenty-one and ruled the kingdom of Judah from Jerusalem for eleven years, as recorded in 2 Kings 24:18. According to 2 Kings 25:7, Zedekiah met a tragic end; his sons were executed before his eyes, after which he was blinded, shackled in bronze fetters, and taken captive to Babylon. This event signifies the end of the line of Judean kings.

Zedekiah's reign began in Adar (March) of 598 BCE and ended on the 9th of

Tammuz in 587 BCE. Babylonian historical records confirm that the Babylonians exiled Jehoiachin and his family to Babylon in February of 598 BCE. According to the prophet Jeremiah, Zedekiah's escape from Jerusalem took place in Tammuz, which corresponds to the end of June in 587 BCE, exactly one month before the destruction of Jerusalem and the Temple by fire.

The Exile

The Babylonian Exile was a profoundly challenging time in Jewish history. During this difficult period, many Judeans from the ancient Kingdom of Judah were forcibly displaced from their homeland and relocated to Babylonia by the Neo-Babylonian Empire.

This concludes the study of Israel and Judah's kings from the division of the kingdom until the defeats of Israel and Judah.

John Ferris

CHAPTER 9

Analysis of the Chronological Framework of the Monarchical Period in Israel and Judah

The longstanding debate surrounding the reconciliation of the reign durations of the thirty nine monarchs of Israel and Judah, along with thirty two cross references from the Masoretic Text (MT) and two from the Septuagint (LXX), has resulted in the task being declared impossible. However, recent analyses reveal a remarkable alignment within this chronology, indicating that any attempt to adjust the reign durations would significantly compromise the integrity of the reconciliation process.

Charts showing the reigns of the Divided Kingdom highlight the challenges of changing the Hebrew timeline. The years from 952 to 726 BCE are linked through detailed references, creating a straightforward narrative. Altering any historical details would require significant revisions to these charts, which would be difficult to justify.

The data in these charts matches the accounts in the books of Kings and Chronicles. Instead of showing contradictions, these sources often present paradoxes that challenge straightforward interpretations. The interesting part is figuring out how to understand and resolve these complexities.

This development will likely receive support from two main groups: scholars across various fields engaged in historical research and individuals of faith, especially those from Jewish and Christian backgrounds, who may find comfort in confirming that scriptural accounts serve as reliable sources for the chronology of the monarchy. Conversely, those focused on defending their personal, academic, or institutional reputations are likely to feel discontent.

Sceptics of these findings must offer alternative charts that can adequately reflect the lengths of reign of the thirty nine monarchs and demonstrate the fidelity of the thirty four cross references. When hypotheses lack strong foundations, the alternative representations often appear as vague outlines that fail to highlight inconvenient data.

Summary of the Examination of the Divided Kingdom

The fully reconciled figures from the Books of Kings and Chronicles clearly illustrate the relationships between the reigns of the kingdoms of Judah and Israel during the period from 952 to 722 BCE. The organisation of these 230 years effectively utilises a framework of thirty four cross references.

Throughout this period, there were nineteen reigns in Israel and thirteen in Judah, from Rehoboam to Hezekiah, that fitted precisely into the chart. This chart compiles the reigns and reveals no internal contradictions or missing synchronisms. The tractate *Rosh Hashanah*, written around 190 to 230 CE, outlines the principles used to arrange the reigns and accurately describes the accession system that defines them. The data is so closely connected that attempting to manipulate the figures will compromise the document's integrity.

Additionally, researchers have dismissed the notion of dual dating or relying on timelines from neighbouring nations. Aside from the interaction between Jehoiachin and Nebuchadnezzar, which established a key reference point, no external information was necessary to deduce the absolute timeline of the Divided Kingdom.

By avoiding the tools used by scholars like Thiele and Ussher, the essential element required to solve this puzzle was determining a set of assumptions that would satisfy all the requirements for resolving the substantial dataset that has challenged generations of academics.

The ultimate test for the absolute timeline is in its application to synchronisms with other nations. So far, the Hebrew timeline that has emerged as a result of this study has helped identify errors in the Assyrian and Egyptian timelines.

Critique of Thiele's Model

As Edwin Thiele wisely noted:

"The chronologist must keep in mind that it is not his task to manufacture history but to recover history. In dealing with chronology, he is dealing with something fundamental and absolute, something absolutely fixed that allows no deviation in any way, even by a single year, if it is to be entirely correct. If the chronologist's work cannot meet this test of absolute harmony with all else that is sound, then at some point the work is in error. The work has not been completed and must be started again in order to discover error, correct the mistakes, and keep on till harmony is achieved." (Thiele, 1983:7)

Although Thiele's ambitious goals inspire hope for completely reliable results, his foundational assumptions have prevented him from achieving the absolute timeline he envisioned. His primary mistakes were trusting the reliability of the Assyrian timeline and assuming that his understanding of the reigns of Sargon II and Sennacherib was accurate.

The Assyrian Synchronisms

The Significance of the Neo Assyrian Empire

Historians traditionally consider the Neo Assyrian Empire to have existed from 911 BCE until 609 BCE. In light of the previous discussion regarding the twenty one year reign of Shammuramat, it becomes necessary to substantiate the assertion regarding the years that have been expunged from both the Assyrian King List and the Assyrian Eponym List. Our analysis proposes revising the chronology to encompass 932 BCE to 611 BCE.

In juxtaposition, the Divided Kingdoms of Israel and Judah frame the Assyrian timeline, with the Kingdom of Israel lasting from 952 BCE until its downfall in 722 BCE and the Kingdom of Judah enduring until 587 BCE. During the formidable reigns of David and Solomon, Assyria had diminished to a secondary regional power. However, within two decades of the division of the kingdoms, Assyria experienced a revival, engaging in a series of interactions with Israel and Judah throughout the Neo Assyrian period. The Assyrians documented every perceived triumph in stone inscriptions and clay tablets, often prioritizing their narratives over historical accuracy, while Hebrew texts recorded their defeats and victories.

The Assyrian Eponym Lists: An Overview

Since the mid nineteenth century, numerous copies of clay fragments have been unearthed, allowing for the reconstruction of what are understood to be the official annual records of the Assyrian Empire. These lists, known as the Assyrian Eponym Lists, are of significant historical importance as they document what is erroneously assumed to be an unbroken chronological account spanning from 892 to 648 BCE. The methodology employed in these recordings involved high ranking officials providing their names, titles, and succinct descriptions of significant events that transpired in the preceding year.

The eponymous system, a cornerstone of the Assyrian Empire, significantly influenced the governance and representation of the state. One influential elucidation of this system posits that the sequence commenced with the king, followed in rotation by various high officials. These included the *tartan*, who served as commander in chief and represented the military, followed by the *niru ekali*, or chief of the palace, who acted as the principal representative of the state. The next in line was the *rab bitur*, the head of the priesthood, representing the nation's religious affairs, followed by the *tukulu*, a military officer attached to the king.

Collectively, these four officials, along with the king, constituted the principal eponymes and epitomes of the governing body of the Assyrian state. Following this core group, the eponymous roles were filled by governors of prominent cities, with the general governor or head prefect presiding over these appointments.

Notably, the official arrangement of the eponyms was not fixed and sometimes exhibited variations, highlighting the dynamic and evolving nature of Assyrian governance. For instance, following Sargon's accession, notable irregularities began to emerge within the system. His successor, Sennacherib, appears to have deviated from tradition by postponing his participation in the eponymous rotation until the eighteenth year of his reign.

This act marked a significant departure from established customs, leading to a phase in which governors, generals, and court officials predominantly received the eponymy. No subsequent monarchs engaged in the practice (Smith, 1875). A surprising development emerges when we reexamine Sennacherib's portion of the list.

This book later supports the idea that Sargon II and Sennacherib were coregents from the beginning of Sargon II's reign in 721/720 BCE. Within the Assyrian regnal framework, people observed a jubilee every thirty years, a significant event marking the completion of a monarch's thirty year reign. When a monarch ruled for more than thirty years, the established sequence of eponyms would recur, with the king being honoured shortly after completing his thirtieth year.

Shalmaneser III is the sole Assyrian king to have surpassed the thirty year mark, receiving an eponym in both his first and thirty first years of rule. Given that Sennacherib had already completed a fifteen year tenure as coregent prior to the death of Sargon II in 705 BCE, the conclusion of the eighteenth year following the commencement of his sole reign would correspond to the thirty third year of his combined period of rule. This fulfilled the criteria for recognition in the Assyrian

Eponym List associated with the thirty year jubilee.

It is important to note that Sargon II's eponymous year was 719/718 BCE, two years after he began his reign. Sennacherib's eponymous year occurred thirty one years after Sargon's, following the pattern established by Shalmaneser III.

An Analytical Overview of the Assyrian Eponym Chart

It is essential to clarify that the blank spaces within the chart displayed on the next page do not signify absent eponyms or missing years. Instead, these blanks were deliberately created to allow for vertical spacing of certain groups of titles, thereby facilitating a horizontal alignment that highlights prevailing patterns within the data.

One significant factor that disrupted the regular cycle of eponyms was the demise or replacement of officials occupying the four principal positions subordinate to the king. When new appointees took office, they were often immediately designated as limmu, or eponym, for that calendar year.

The majority of titles were consistently used throughout the timeline. This consistency reflects a certain level of predictability, as some governors rose in rank while others fell. Occasionally, new titles emerged while older ones disappeared.

The Assyrians sought to mitigate the likelihood of individuals receiving a second eponymate in close succession to their first. In cases where a king's reign was brief, it was customary for the heir to continue his father's established pattern, often integrating his name alongside that of his commander in chief.

When two consecutive reigns of short duration occurred, the third sovereign always initiated a fresh pattern. Historical evidence shows that when a king reigned for more than thirty years, he reinstated the cyclical pattern of the chart as close as possible to the thirtieth year of his reign.

ASSYRIAN EPONYM LIST BY REIGN

Shalmaneser III 879/78 – 844/43	Shamsi-adad V 843/42 – 831/30	Shammuramat 830/29 – 810/09	Adad-nirai III 809/08 – 782/81	Shalmaneser IV 781/80 – 772/71	Ashur-dan III 771/70 – 754/53	Ashur-nerari V 753/52 – 746/45	Tiglath-pileser III 745/55 – 728/27
							Gov. of Arrapha
Saru-baltu-nisi							Gov. of Kalah
KING	KING	QUEEN	KING	KING	KING	KING	KING
Commander	Commander	Commander	Commander	Commander	Commander	Commander	Commander
Chief Butler	Palace Herald		Palace Herald	Chief Butler		Palace Herald	Palace Herald
Palace Herald	Chamberlain?		Chief Butler	Palace Herald		Chief Butler	Chief Butler
Commander	Gov. of Assur?		Chamberlain	Chamberlain		Chamberlain	Chamberlain
	Gov. of Isana		Gov. of Assur	Gov. of Assur		Gov. of Assur	Gov. of Assur
	Chief Butler		Gov. Rasapha	Gov. Rasapha		Gov. Rasapha	Gov. Rasapha
Gov. of Nisibin	Gov. of Nisibin		Gov. of Arrapha	Gov. of Nisibin			Gov. of Nisibin
	Commander		Gov. Ahizuhina	Gov. of Raqmat	Gov. of Arrapha		Gov. of Arrapha
Gov. of Kalah			Gov. of Nisibin	Gov. of Kalah			Gov. of Kalah
Palace Herald			Gov. of Amedi		Gov. of Zamua		Gov. of Zamua
Gov. of Nairi			Chamberlain				Gov. of Simme
Gov. of Assur?	Gov. of Habruri		Gov. of Kalah		Gov. Ahizuhina		Gov. Ahizuhina
Gov. of Arrapha?	Gov. of Raqmat				Gov. of Tille		Gov. of Tille
Gov. of Zamua?	Gov. of Arrapha						
Gov. of Tille?	Gov. of Zamua	???	Gov. of Habruri		Gov. of Habruri		Gov. of Habruri
Gov. Tushhan?		???	Gov. of Raqmat		Gov. of Tushhan		Gov. of Tushhan
Gov. Shibhinish?		Tushhan?	Gov. of Tushhan		Gov. of Guzana		Gov. of Guzana
G. Hemed-Ishtar		Guzana?	Gov. of Guzana		Gov. of Amedi		Gov. of Amedi
Gov. of Guzana		Tille?	Gov. of Tille			Shalmaneser V 727/26 - 722/21	
Gov. of Rasapha		Shibhinish?	Gov. Shibhinish				
Gov. of Ahizuhina		Isana?	Gov. of Isana				
Gov. of Raqmat		Nineveh?	Gov. of Nineveh		Gov. of Nineveh		Gov. of Nineveh
Gov. of Habruri		Kilizi?	Gov. of Kilizi		Gov. of Kilizi		Gov. of Kilizi
Gov. of Nineveh		Arbela?	Gov. of Arbela		Gov. of Arbela		KING
Chamberlain		???			Gov. of Isana		Commander
Gov. of Kilizi		Tamnunna?			Gov. of Kurbail		
Gov. of Arbela		Talmasu?	Gov. of Talmasu		Gov. of Tamnunna		
Gov. of Isana		???	Gov. Tamnunna		Gov. Shibhinish		
Gov. Tamnunna?		???	Gov. Arbela		Gov. of Talmasu		
Gov. of Talmasu?		Queen?	Gov. of Zamua				
KING		Commander?	Gov. of Nisibin	The reigns of Sargon II and Sennacherib shall be examined in detail in the next table.			
Commander		???					
Chief Butler		???					
Commander							
Palace Herald							

Even with the complexities involved, there is a noticeable pattern. This predictability allows scholars to make an educated guess about what might be in damaged or unreadable records. These guesses are written in italics and marked with question marks for easy identification.

The coregency of Sargon & Sennacherib		
Sargon II & Sennacherib 721/20 - 682/81		
Title	Date	Count
Palace Herald	721/720	
Governor of ??	720/719	
King Sargon II	719/718	START
Gov. of Rasappa	718/717	1
Chamberlain	717/716	2
Gov. of Libbi-ali	716/715	3
Gov. of Nisibis	715/714	4
Gov. of Arrapha	714/713	5
Gov. of Kalhu	713/712	6
Gov. of Mazamua	712/711	7
Gov. of Si'immel	711/710	8
Gov. of Ahizuhina	710/709	9
Gov. of Tille	709/708	10
Gov. of Habruri	708/707	11
Gov. of Tushan	707/706	12
Gov. of Guzana	706/705	13
Sargon II killed, Sennacherib begins sole reign		
Gov. of Amedi	705/704	14
Gov. of Nineveh	704/703	15
Gov. of Kalizi	703/702	16
Gov. of Arbela	702/701	17
Gov. of Til-barsip	701/700	18
Gov. of Isana	700/699	19
Gov. of Kurba'il	699/698	20
Gov. of Halziatbar	698/697	21
Gov. of Talmasu	697/696	22
Gov. of Shahuppa	696/695	23
Gov. of Damascus	695/694	24
Gov. of Dur-Sharuken	694/693	25
Gov. of Arpad	693/692	26
Gov. of Carcamesh	692/691	27
Gov. of Samaria	691/690	28
Gov. of Hatarikka	690/689	29
Gov. of Simirra	689/688	30
King Sennacherib	688/687	31

Evidence for the Hypothesized Coregency between Sargon II and Sennacherib

Here is the chart demonstrating the reigns of Sargon II and Sennacherib. When compared to the chart for the historical reigns of Assyrian monarchs going back as far as Shalmaneser III, it can be shown that their combined reigns comply closely with the traditional pattern.

While not a single, formal calendar system like our modern Gregorian calendar, the Assyrian system of thirty year cycles is a concept used to understand the broader context of ancient Assyrian timekeeping. It primarily refers to grouping years into cycles of approximately thirty years, which is relevant for understanding the reigns of kings and the organization of historical events.

One example of a reign exceeding thirty years during the Neo Assyrian period is that of Shalmaneser III. His eponyms occurred during his second and thirty first years, the gap being twenty nine years. The Assyrian system allowed for some variation depending on prevailing circumstances.

By the time of Sargon II, the system for organizing the sequence of eponyms had been adhered to with notable precision, with the exception of what seems to be a missing reign. Further discussion on this matter will be provided in a subsequent section.

Various commentators have proposed different theories regarding Sennacherib's apparent discontinuation of the accepted order within the eponymous system. However, many of these analyses overlook a critical interpretation: the hypothesis that Sargon II and Sennacherib acted as coregents from the very beginning of Sargon II's reign. This perspective may provide a coherent explanation for the irregularities observed in the succession of eponyms. Although such an arrangement is unprecedented in the history of Assyria, it is worth noting that this father and son shared a strong and unusual bond.

At this juncture, the hypothesis serves as a preliminary indication of the detailed analysis to be presented in a subsequent section focused on the timeline of Sennacherib. The accompanying chart, which precedes this discussion, represents merely a fraction of the extensive evidence available to substantiate the claim that Sargon II and Sennacherib co reigned equally until the demise of Sargon.

Problems Associated with the Eponym Lists

Assuming that the eponym record is entirely accurate and free of errors or omissions creates significant challenges, especially when using this list as a reference for establishing synchronisms with other historical kingdoms. A thorough examination of the mechanisms and motivations for inaccuracies within the Assyrian timeline will be conducted shortly. Fundamentally, the chronology attributed to events in the first half of the first millennium BCE heavily relies on findings derived from the Assyrian record, which has undergone intentional modifications.

A chart showing the reigns of Neo Assyrian rulers, including Shammuramat, has been created to highlight patterns in the eponym systems.

Earlier in this manuscript, it was noted that the synchronisms established between Shalmaneser III and two Hebrew monarchs occurred twenty one years earlier than

Thiele's assertions. This discrepancy may stem from several possible explanations, the most prominent being either errors of calculation or inaccuracies in Thiele's assumptions regarding the reliability of the Assyrian data. While the calculations alone provide a compelling argument, they are further strengthened by additional corroborative evidence, which is readily observable to those with a talent for discerning patterns within the historical data.

Observations and Deductions Regarding the Eponym Lists

The compilations utilized by Assyriologists and historians, commonly called eponym lists, represent a synthesis of various documents produced at distinct intervals during the Neo Assyrian period. Given the fragmented state of certain records, scholars have integrated information from these disparate sources to construct a relatively comprehensive understanding of the period's historical landscape.

Nevertheless, one must approach the Assyrian records with scepticism, as the accuracy of these accounts often requires validation through contemporaneous records from neighbouring nations with which the Assyrians engaged. The current reconstruction of the Hebrew record demonstrates this point.

Before the advent of the Neo Assyrian period, approximately coinciding with the early stages of the first millennium BCE, the chronology of Assyrian history is marked by at least three distinct versions. Even the canonical eponym lists from the Neo Assyrian era warrant scrutiny, as the adage "leopards do not change their spots" aptly encapsulates the enduring nature of historical revisionism.

The annals of Assyrian history reveal the pervasive influence of royal agendas, wherein monarchs sought to manipulate the historical record to enhance their legacies relative to their predecessors and successors. It seems plausible that the dates of Assyrian reigns remain relatively reliable from Adad nirari III's reign, which commenced in 809/808 BCE. Any dates before that reign appear suspect, as Shammuramat has had most references to her reign deleted from the records.

As elucidated in the preceding chapter, there exists a significant chronologic gap of twenty one years prior to Adad nirari III's rule, a gap strongly believed to correspond with the reign of the only identifiable figure at that juncture—Shamshi Adad V's widow, Shammuramat, recognized as the Warrior Queen of the Assyrians.

This section of the discourse argues that scholars have satisfactorily addressed the complexities surrounding the interpretation of biblical texts in the Books of Kings and Chronicles. This book accurately dates the commencement of the Divided Kingdom to 952 BCE, a figure that comes twenty one years earlier than Thiele's estimate of 931/930 BCE.

The inscriptions of Shalmaneser III, as documented on the Kurkh Stele and the Black Obelisk, which detail his interactions with King Ahab and King Jehu of Israel, present compelling evidence of the events but not the chronology. The twelve year interval unequivocally aligns Ahab's final year (874/873 BCE) with Jehu's accession (862/861 BCE). The dates for the events proposed by Thiele in 1951 are 853 BCE and 841 BCE. There will likely be significant resistance to any questioning of those dates.

By correlating the sixth and eighteenth years of Shalmaneser with significant Hebrew historical milestones about Ahab and Jehu, and subsequently progressing through the eponyms, one arrives at a date of 831/830 BCE, marking the conclusion of Shamsi-adad V's reign.

The twenty-one-year gap between 830/829 and 810/809 BCE suggests an intriguing conclusion: a later king deliberately obliterated many historical records about the reign of Shammuramat. This omission may be due to Tiglath Pileser III, a subsequent king, who would have been overshadowed in history by the accomplishments of the celebrated queen. This ruthless self-promoter exhibited a notable disregard for preceding rulers.

Tiglath Pileser III, who likely came to power by deposing the reigning king, may have been the biological son or brother of King Assur nigari V. Some commentators speculate that Assur nigari V and Tiglath Pileser were coregents for the latter part of Assur nigari's reign.

A Critical Examination of the Assyrian King List during the Period of the Divided Kingdom

The examination reveals significant insights into the reigns of Ashur Dan II (954/53 – 932/31), Adad nerari II (931/30 – 911/10), and Tukulti ninurta II (910/09 – 904/03). Over fifty years, the available Assyrian records document the succession of these monarchs and their officials; however, they include formal titles on only a few occasions.

This trend aligns with the practices of the Middle Assyrian Period, beginning with King Eriba ada I around 1400 BCE and continuing through to Ashur Dan II, whose death is estimated to have occurred in 932/31 BCE. The scarcity of titles in the historical record hinders a comprehensive understanding of the eponymous patterns during this era.

Assur nasirpal II (circa 903/02 – 880/79 BCE):

He presided over a significant twenty-four-year reign. Notably, this king's eponym year occupies the foremost position in the chronological records, including two and potentially three additional titles. The records attribute the limmu mentioned in his ninth year to the Governor of Kalah. This finding aligns with subsequent reigns wherein Kalah frequently appears around the tenth year of various rulers.

In the eponym list, the figure Qurdi ashur appears in the tenth position. While his official title is not explicitly stated, it is pertinent to point out that a contemporary bearing the same name served as the Governor of Raqmat during the nineteenth year of Shalmaneser III, approximately thirty-seven years later. It is plausible that this individual experienced a decline in favour under the new regime, as the governorship of Raqmat exhibited variability under successive kings.

Additionally, the Governor of Tushhan is recorded in the fifteenth position, reflecting a continuity with the later Governors of Tushhan roles. During Assur nasirpal II's reign, this arrangement within the eponym positioning establishes a precedent that later Assyrian monarchs echo in their patterns of eponym hierarchy.

Shalmaneser III (879/78 – 844/43): An Examination of Eponymous Years and Administrative Transition

Shalmaneser III's extensive reign, spanning thirty-five years, encompassed notable disruptions to the established cycle of eponymous years. Particularly noteworthy are the occurrences in his nineteenth and twentieth years, during which the eponymous governorships of Rassapha and Ahizuhina underwent an unusual shift.

After the governors Samas abua of Rassapha and Sulma beli lamar of Ahizuhina were replaced, officials appointed new individuals who received eponymous years in the twenty-first and twenty-second years of Shalmaneser's reign. This deviation from standard protocol may suggest underlying political actions involving the aforementioned governors, potentially executed on behalf of or against the reigning monarch.

Eponymous status is usually conferred promptly on the most critical positions within the realm, such as the King and the Commander in Chief. However, certain high-ranking officials such as the Palace Herald, Chief Butler, and Chamberlain could be similarly acknowledged, albeit not universally.

The status of Rassapha improved significantly, as evidenced by its elevation to the seventh position in subsequent reigns. In the twenty-fifth year of Shalmaneser III, the appointment of Yahulu as Chamberlain marks a significant development, particularly in light of the absence of any recorded chamberlain in the earlier years of Shalmaneser's rule. The likely scenario is that a previous chamberlain had either died or been replaced towards the conclusion of Assur nasirpal II's reign, leading to the conferral of an eponymy upon the newly appointed Chamberlain.

During that historical period, people recorded the names of eponyms, but many officials did not document their titles.

Throughout his reign, Shalmaneser III presided over three commanders in chief. Assur bela ka'in, the Commander at the commencement of Shalmaneser's reign, was succeeded by Dayan assur in the thirty-second year. It is plausible that the political instability marked by a civil revolt, which afflicted the final four years of Shalmaneser III's rule, resulted in the demise of both commanders. Upon the death of Dayan assur, Yahulu ascended from his position as Chamberlain to become Commander in Chief of the military.

Given the protracted duration of Shalmaneser III's reign, the cycle of eponyms experienced a renewal, with Shalmaneser himself assuming his second eponymous year in the thirty-first year of his governance. He was succeeded in eponymous status by the Commander in Chief, the Chief Butler, another Commander in Chief, and the Palace Herald.

This examination of the eponymous years under Shalmaneser III explains the complicated politics and changes in administration during this time.

Shamsi adad V (843/42 – 831/30):

He ascended to the throne following the death of Shalmaneser III, inheriting a kingdom embroiled in civil strife, primarily instigated by his brother, Assur danin pal. The authorities successfully quelled the unrest by the third year of his reign.

During Shamsi adad V's tenure, he designated three eponyms for critical positions: the King, the Commander in Chief (named Yahulu), and a newly appointed Palace Herald. The previous Palace Herald had likely perished during the aforementioned revolt. This allocation accounts for three top eponym positions, leaving two to elucidate.

Assur bunaya usur, the Chief Butler, held his eponym toward the conclusion of Shalmaneser's reign. The officials postponed the recognition of Assur bunaya usur as an eponym until the seventh year of Shamsi adad's reign due to the proximity of these events. Yahulu's promotion from Chamberlain to Commander in Chief occurred in Shalmaneser's penultimate year, which required appointing a new Chamberlain. The unfolding events would determine the identity of this new Chamberlain.

After the initial three eponyms, we observe signs of damage or wear on the records of the two subsequent eponyms, which makes them less legible. Given the relatively predictable nature of eponym cycles, it is reasonable to speculate that these positions corresponded to the titles Chamberlain and Governor of Assur. The names associated with these titles are known to be Inurta ubla and Samas ilaya, respectively.

Remarkably, the Governor of Isana achieved an elevated rank, attaining the sixth position during Shamsi adad's reign. Typically, kings classified Isana as a low ranking city, often placing it around the twentieth rank. This exceptional promotion suggests that the governor and the city played a significant role during the king's tumultuous years, notably as twenty seven cities in Assyria, including Nineveh, rallied in opposition.

The governor, Nergal ilaya, is documented as holding limmu status on three occasions: twice as Governor of Isana during the twenty eighth year of Shalmaneser III and in the sixth year of Shamsi adad, and subsequently as Commander in Chief during the second year of Adad nirari III. Notably, if one includes the twenty one year tenure of Shammuramat as Queen Regent, the interval between the first and third eponyms of Nergal ilaya spans an impressive forty three years. While seemingly excessive, this duration is further contextualized by the even lengthier tenure of his successor, Samsi ilu, as Commander in Chief.

Queen Shammuramat (830/29 – 810/09): An Examination of Her Tenure and Historical Context

The reign of Queen Shammuramat as Queen Regent invites significant scholarly discourse, particularly concerning Thiele's and his adherents' prevailing convictions regarding the integrity of the Assyrian chronological narrative as derived from eponymous chronicles. This discourse necessitates critically examining the assertions surrounding Shammuramat's purported twenty one year reign.

Several key arguments emerge regarding the chronological markers linked to Shammuramat's governance. Firstly, a discernible twenty one year interval arises when aligning the dates of Shalmaneser III's engagements with the Israelite monarchs Ahab and Jehu against the absolute chronology of the Divided Kingdom, as delineated in earlier sections of this work.

Furthermore, it is imperative to consider the circumstances surrounding Adad nirari III, who ascended the throne as an infant following the death of his father, Shamsi adad V. The length of Adad nirari's reign—twenty eight years—poses a theoretical quandary; without the intervention of a regent, he would have been no more than thirty years of age at his demise. The historical records do not reference Shalmaneser IV assuming power as a youthful ruler. Thus, recognizing Shammuramat's twenty one year regency provides a plausible explanation for these discrepancies.

Historically, Shammuramat, often called "The Warrior Queen of Assyria," is credited with considerable achievements. Suppose one were to accept claims of her approximately forty year rule. In that case, it is reasonable to postulate that the initial twenty one years transpired under her governance, with the latter part spent in partnership with Adad nirari III as coregent once he reached maturity.

Moreover, contemporary Assyrian sources from the ninth century, including eponym lists and chronicles, which date from the seventh century, do not mention Shammuramat. However, the discovery of her royal stele, positioned among the limmu stelae at Assur, indicates her formal appointment as limmu. This contemporary inscription carries greater significance than the later copies and updates that characterize revised eponym lists and chronicles.

Furthermore, if Adad nirari III's rule had immediately succeeded Shamsi adad V's, we would anticipate a different arrangement of the eponymous officiators. Given Shamsi adad V's thirteen year reign, the subsequent appointment of a new king and Commander in Chief would typically occur, followed by a continuation of the existing eponymic cycle. Instead, the records reflect a systematic restart of this cycle, supporting the assertion that Shammuramat maintained the administrative structures established during her husband's reign.

Considering the brevity of Shamsi adad V's tenure, one must inquire into the continuity of office bearers at the time of Adad nirari III's accession. Evidence suggests that only one official, Nergal ilaya, remained active in office, a figure consistent with expectations if Queen Shammuramat served as Queen Regent for the hypothesized twenty one year period. This extended term accounts for the anticipated attrition rate of officials.

In conclusion, the complexities surrounding Queen Shammuramat's rule warrant further investigation, particularly in light of Assyrian history's historical, administrative, and chronological discrepancies.

Adad nirari III (809/08 – 782/81):

During this period of governance, there was a notable adherence to the established protocols that characterized the political landscape. The appointments of the Governors of Ahizuhina and Amedi suggest a deliberate elevation within the hierarchical structure, likely serving as a form of commendation for their loyal service to the crown. This transient promotion may reflect the broader socio political dynamics at play and the strategic maneuvering often observed in royal administrations.

Shalmaneser IV (781/80 – 772/71):

During this period, we observe a unique shift from the expected normative structure. Notably, the Governor of Raqmat assumed the ranking traditionally associated with the Governor of Arrapha, leading to an interesting transformation in the established hierarchies.

Ashur-dan III (771/70 – 754/53):

He presided over a notable period within the Assyrian chronological framework, particularly concerning the arrangement of eponyms. Scholars have speculated about the potential deletion of eponyms from the early portion of his reign; however, a detailed analysis of the eponymous patterns reveals that such claims are unfounded.

The brevity of Shalmaneser IV's ten-year reign necessitated the insertion of Ashur dan III's eponym and his Commander in Chief before resuming the eponymic sequence established initially by his father. Consequently, the eponym for the Governor of Arrapha, displaced during the preceding monarchy, emerged as the subsequent entry in the eponymic list, following the King and the Commander in Chief.

The latter part of Ashur dan III's reign illustrates a consistent cycle of eponym appointments that adhered to anticipated patterns. According to the eponym canon, the year 765 witnessed a significant plague afflicting Assyria, which hindered the king's military campaigns the following year. By 763, a revolt erupted, persisting until 759, when another plague again beset the land.

This tumultuous era, characterized by internal strife and periodic epidemic disease, has led to speculation that the biblical figure Jonah visited Nineveh at this time of unrest, resulting in a temporary mass conversion of its populace to worship the God of the Hebrews. The Book of Jonah claims this, but no Assyrian records confirm it.

Ashur nerari V (753/52 – 746/45):

The pattern of eponyms during this period exhibited a conservative nature, devoid of any remarkable deviations. Assyria experienced a decline in centralization, with significant powers devolving to the governors of various cities.

It is posited that Shammuramat strategically relinquished certain central authorities to enhance her political favor and garner support for her reign through the empowerment of these governors. Furthermore, it is suggested that Tiglath Pileser III, confronted with the obstinacy of Ashur nerari V, ultimately deposed him in a bid to wind back the powers devolved to governors and restore authority to the Assyrian throne.

It is likely that Ashur nerari V and Tiglath Pileser III were coregents for much of his reign.

Tiglath Pileser III (745/44 – 728/27):

He is often considered to have usurped the throne from his predecessor, which may have served as a historical example for the actions of Judah's King Ahaz, who deposed his father Jotham in 734 BCE. Tiglath Pileser appears to have garnered substantial support from the city of Kalhu (also called Calah or Kalah, corresponding to modern day Nimrud).

Tiglath -pileser III of Assyria captures the city of Astartu. An Assyrian soldier waving a mace escorts four deportees with sacks over their shoulders ca. 730-727 BCE. The final deportations occurred in 722 BCE under Shalmaneser V.

Historical records indicate that he was governor over a northern city, with a prevailing consensus among scholars suggesting that this city was indeed Kalhu. Notably, the record for 746/45 reflects a revolt occurring within Kalhu.

Tiglath Pileser ascended the throne in the subsequent year. Typically, a king would serve as the eponym for the first year of his reign. However, it appears that Tiglath Pileser intentionally chose to perpetuate the established eponymate pattern of his predecessor for an additional two years.

This decision likely aimed to honor the governor of Kalhu, whose eponym year was imminent. The eponyms for the inaugural two years of Tiglath Pileser's reign corresponded to the Governor of Arrapha, followed by that of Kalhu.

Shalmaneser V (727/26 – 722/21):

Shalmaneser V, the successor of Tiglath Pileser III, faced considerable challenges stemming from his father's contentious legacy, particularly regarding the unpopular reintroduction of taxes on the sacred cities of Ashur and Harran.

The ruins of Samaria as recorded in 1839

He adhered to the traditional eponymous administrative cycle during his reign, maintaining it for four years before assuming the eponymate himself in the fifth year of his rule. Notably, during Shalmaneser V's tenure, the siege of Samaria commenced.

He ultimately passed away around 722/21 BCE, following the defeat of Samaria. However, the subsequent ruler, Sargon II, claimed credit well after the event for completing this military endeavor. The historical record, particularly through inscriptions, provides a limited understanding of Shalmaneser V's reign and contributions, rendering him a somewhat enigmatic figure in the annals of Assyrian history.

Sargon II (721/20 – 706/05) and Sennacherib (705/04 – 682/81):

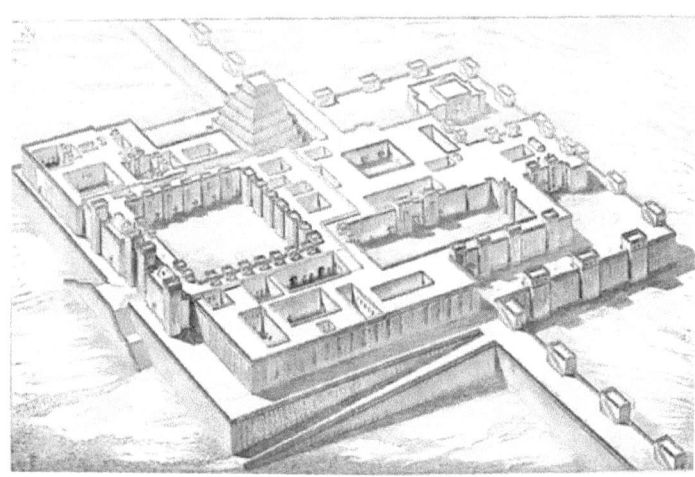

Reconstructed Model of Palace of Sargon at Khorsabad 1905

Skepticism about Sargon II's historical existence persisted until the mid-nineteenth century, specifically the 1840s, when the French Consul General in Mosul, Paul Émile Botta, uncovered the site of Sargon's temple, conducting excavations between 1842 and 1844. Before this discovery, the mention of Sargon was confined to a single biblical reference, leading some skeptics to dismiss it as an aberration or error within the scriptural narratives.

Sargon II adhered closely to the eponymous chronological framework, a practice continued by his coregent, Sennacherib, who ascended to the throne as sole king following Sargon's death. Sennacherib embraced the eponymous tradition and significantly modified the methodology of documenting his accomplishments.

Instead of recording events sequentially by year of reign, he chronicled them by the sequence of major military campaigns. His annals, notably inscribed on Sennacherib's Prism, recount eight campaigns.

Few scholars support the Ussherite doctrine, which proposes that Sargon II and Sennacherib were the same person. The Book of Tobit (1:18) lends credence to this idea by naming Sennacherib the son of Shalmaneser V. This book suggests that there was a prolonged coregency between Sargon II and Sennacherib and that Sennacherib's military campaigns were retellings of joint campaigns involving him and his father.

In contrast, other scholars, including Thiele, argue that Sennacherib's eight campaigns began during his sole reign around 705/704 BCE.

Sargon II exhibited a propensity for embellishing his achievements. Analysis of historical records indicates that while Shalmaneser V had effectively subdued Samaria in 722 BCE before his demise in early 721 BCE, Sargon II later claimed credit for this victory, albeit only recording it in his annals in the fifteenth or sixteenth year of his reign.

The detailed accounts in Sargon's records and his campaigns against Judah from 715 to 714 BCE lack substantive clarity. In contrast, Sennacherib's chronicles emphasized his victories, boasting of his conquering 46 cities and imposing substantial tributes upon Hezekiah.

Interestingly, Sennacherib deliberately omitted the repercussions of military setbacks, a common practice reflective of a culture that prioritized celebrating triumphs while rarely acknowledging failures.

Given that both Sargon II and Sennacherib's records are imbued with elements of royal vanity and may manipulate historical accuracy, as noted by Luckenbill in 1926, historians and biblical scholars have encountered significant challenges in reconciling the discrepancies between these records and the biblical narrative.

Sargon's predilection for retrospective claims regarding victories raises pertinent questions about the legitimacy and chronological precision of his purported accomplishments. Prioritizing the solidified biblical timeline may be more beneficial than attempting to align biblical events with Assyrian chronicles, as

Thiele did.

The extant prisms documenting Sennacherib's campaigns, produced approximately fifteen years after Sargon's death, suggest that Sennacherib struggled to maintain a coherent military agenda during his independent reign. This perspective challenges Thiele's viewpoint and highlights how those who overlook Sennacherib's records miss the opportunity to see them as a reinterpretation and appropriation of the joint military campaigns he undertook with his father.

In a later chapter, we provide detailed comparative analyses of the campaigns of Sargon II and Sennacherib, demonstrating that both records recount parallel historical events.

CHAPTER 10

The historical interactions between the Assyrian Empire and the Hebrew kingdoms:

They reveal a complex dynamic that is noteworthy for its scarcity of biblical references prior to the mid 8th century BCE. Despite the absence of mentions in the Scriptures, the Assyrians meticulously chronicled their conquests and administration of the region, providing a wealth of inscriptions that detail these interactions.

Notably, nine rulers from the kingdoms of Israel and Judah are documented within Assyrian records. Among these, five kings—Menachem, Pekah, Hosea, Ahaz, and Hezekiah—are corroborated by parallel accounts in biblical texts. Conversely, the inscriptions concerning the remaining four kings pertain to historical events not addressed within the biblical narrative, thus enhancing our understanding of these particular Israelite monarchs.

This interplay between Assyrian records and biblical accounts serves as a critical point of examination for scholars seeking to delineate the geopolitical landscape of the ancient Near East (Wood, 2012). Following are the recorded interactions:

Ahab and Jehu represent the initial two monarchs among the quartet referenced. Their respective synchronisms with the sixth and eighteenth years of Shalmaneser III align with the revised chronological framework, specifically corresponding to the years 874/873 BCE and 862/861 BCE. Most sources rely on Thiele's dates of 853 and 841 respectively. This temporal correlation underscores the significance of these kings in establishing an absolute chronology.

Jehoash of Israel: The next synchronism is that recorded by Adad nirari III on a stele found at Tell al Rimah in 1967. Tetley observes, "The AEC [Assyrian Eponym Canon] exhibits another inconsistency between Assyrian and biblical records, again during Adad nirari III's reign. The problem concerns the synchronisation of Adad nirari's 5th year with the payment of tribute by Joash I. In current chronologies [e.g. Thiele et al.], Joash I is not contemporaneous with Adad nirari's 5th year. Briefly, the situation is as follows. The Assyrian Tell al Rimah Stela records a western campaign by Adad nirari undertaken in a single year in which Mari' of Damascus, Jehoash of Samaria (i.e. Joash I), and the king of Tyre and Sidon paid him tribute. The Saba'a Stela attributes to Adad nirari's 5th year a western campaign and submission of rebel kings..." (Tetley, 2005:99).

According to the generally accepted AEC dates, the fifth year of Adad nirari III would be 805/804. From the calculations of the reign of Joash/Jehoash of Israel, his regnal dates are 819n – 803n. In the model elucidated in this book, Adad nirari and Joash's synchronism is confirmed.

On pages 112 and 113 of MNHK, Thiele attempts (unsuccessfully) to explain away the contradiction to his model, whereby his figure for the beginning of Joash's reign at 798, seven years adrift of Adad nirari's account. He has once again failed to substantiate his core assumption that one can use Assyrian chronology to make sense of his interpretation of the Hebrew Scriptures.

In his efforts to justify his timeline, he has mentioned the Saba'a Stela by name but has left out vital information that would damage his argument. "Thiele thus declines to provide all the relevant information at his disposal. To have done so affords more years to the Assyrian chronology than Thiele allowed based on the AEC and indicates a serious discrepancy in his chronology" (Tetley, 2005:102).

Thiele first published his book in 1951, and the discovery of the stele at Tell al Rimah in 1967 forced him to produce a second edition in 1970 to minimise the damage to his reputation by this embarrassing discovery. In a classic example of spin, Thiele (1983:111, 112) acknowledged the stele's discovery in 1967, assigned a date of 796 for the interaction, and pretended that this damaging contradiction referred to a later event. In biblical archaeology, the standards for academic reliability may differ from those in other fields. It appears that the Thiele model has not consistently met the basic criteria.

Manasseh of Judah: "Due to his exceptionally protracted reign, Manasseh occupied the throne throughout the entirety of Esarhaddon's rule and for approximately half of Ashurbanipal's reign, both of whom are regarded as formidable monarchs of the Assyrian Empire. Historical records indicate that Manasseh is referenced in the annals of both kings. Notably, he was one of 22 sovereigns mandated to supply construction materials for the royal palace of Esarhaddon in Nineveh" (Wood, 2012).

The chronology of Manasseh's reign, however, holds minimal relevance for the broader timeline, thus necessitating no further exploration in this context.

An Assyrian Queen and Her Place in History: Shammuramat

The Unnamed Savior of Israel:

"And Jehoahaz besought the Lord, and the Lord hearkened unto him; for he saw the oppression of Israel because the king of Syria oppressed them. And the Lord gave Israel a savior so that they went out from under the hand of the Syrians; and the children of Israel dwelt in their tents, as beforetime" (2 Kings 13:4-5).

Many scholars speculate that Israel's savior was Assyria, which intervened through warfare with Syria, relieving the pressure on Israel. A detailed reading of the chapter indicates that the salvation of Israel occurred towards the end of Jehoahaz's reign.

Based on the calculations revealed in this book, Jehoahaz reigned from 833 to 816 BCE. During this period, the monarch of Assyria was Queen Shammuramat, whose reign is estimated to have been from 830/829 to 810/809 BCE. This is the only instance in which we can align a biblical event with her reign.

Research has identified a gap period between the reign of Shamsi-adad V and the official reign of Adad-nirari III. This observation aligns with Tetley's findings: "The problem of only 36 years in the AEC between Shalmaneser's 18th year and Adad-nirari's 5th year points to the AEC's deficiency in this area of eponyms. Any missing eponyms must have fallen from either the end of Shalmaneser's reign or sometime during the reign of Shamshi-adad V. The first five eponyms of Adad-nirari's reign are reasonably certain, as his 5th-year campaign 'to Arpad' occurs against the 5th eponym of his reign. The 36 years of Shalmaneser's reign seem assured because in his 30th eponym, the king again has an eponymate followed by those of his chief officials. Unless eponyms fell from Shalmaneser's reign after his 36th year, they must have fallen during the reign of Shamshi-adad V" (Tetley, 2005, p. 102).

Tetley also notes that at least eight eponym records are missing, and possibly more. We propose a gap of precisely twenty-one years, occurring after the end of Shamsi-adad V's reign. When he died, his son was an infant and, therefore, not in a position to rule. This book suggests that Shammu-ramat, his widow, wielded extraordinary influence in the Assyrian court. She was a skilled politician and negotiator who adeptly maneuvered her way into power with the assistance of formidable allies.

The ascendance of Shammu-ramat to a position of power within the Assyrian empire represents a significant deviation from the predominant gender norms of her time. Long before the reign of Tiglath-pileser III in 745 BCE, there had been a transfer of authority traditionally held by the king to court officials and governors. This redistribution of power likely necessitated specific accommodations, suggesting that a delicate balance of interests was achieved prior to the relinquishing of these royal prerogatives.

Given the deeply ingrained misogyny of Assyrian society, the prospect of a woman exercising authority over men was generally deemed inconceivable. Notably,

Shammu-ramat, of exceptional capability, was one of the few women who dared to aspire to a significant position, ultimately taking on the role of Queen Regent.

Queen Shammu-ramat mourning the death of Ara the Handsome, King of Armenia.

Historian Gwendolyn Leick underscores the remarkable influence Shammuramat wielded within the Assyrian court, noting her ability to erect inscribed monuments in the ceremonial hub of Assur. Leick states, "This woman achieved remarkable fame and power in her lifetime and beyond... She even accompanied her husband on a military campaign, a most unusual undertaking for an Assyrian queen" (Leick, 2009, p. 155). An obelisk inscribed in her name further encapsulates her status:

"Stele of Shammuramat, queen of Shamshi-Adad, King of the Universe, King of Assyria, Mother of Adad Nirari, King of the Universe, King of Assyria, Daughter-in-Law of Shalmaneser, King of the Four Regions of the World."

In addition, historian Stephen Bertman notes that prior to Shamshi-Adad's death,

Shammu-ramat "took the extraordinary step of accompanying her husband on at least one military campaign, and she is prominently mentioned in royal inscriptions" (Bertman, 2005, p. 102). Following his death, it appears that she maintained her influential role and assumed leadership over military campaigns. However, the extent of her direct involvement has been subject to scholarly debate.

The influence of Nergal-ilaya and Samsi-ilu:

During the late 9th to mid 8th centuries BCE, a select group of officials in the Assyrian Empire significantly consolidated their power, posing a considerable challenge to the absolutism of the Assyrian monarchy. Prominent leaders like Samsi-ilu and Nergal-ilaya played influential roles, which recent archaeological findings have illuminated and are now well documented in Assyrian historical studies. The underlying causes for the emergence of such powerful officials during this tumultuous period have been explored in depth, suggesting that their ascendancy represents a direct challenge to the established authority of the Assyrian kings (Grayson, 1992, p. 19).

Nergal-ilaya served as the Governor of Isana during the reign of Shalmaneser III, with his eponymous year recorded as the 28th year of that sovereign's rule. Isana at this time was considered a relatively minor city; however, under the reign of Shamsi-adad V, it experienced a noteworthy elevation to the sixth position in the Assyrian hierarchy. This rise likely reflects the city's and Nergal-ilaya's performance in quelling a rebellion that persisted for six years. Their successful defence of the monarchy during the transitions of power implies a loyalty that would have been crucial in maintaining stability.

After his governorship, Nergal-ilaya served as the commander in chief, as recorded in the Assyrian Eponym List during the second year of Adad-nirari III. He died shortly thereafter, paving the way for Samsi-ilu to rise to power the following year. However, the Eponym List did not document this transition until the reign of

Shalmaneser IV, which occurred about twenty-seven years later.

The eponym chronicle records Samsi-ilu as limmu on three distinct occasions, specifically in the years 780/79, 770/69, and 752/51, correlating his service with three different Assyrian kings: Shalmaneser IV, Ashur-dan III, and Ashur-nirari V, respectively. This chronicle establishes a career timeline for Samsi-ilu that spans from at least 780 to 751 BCE. Scholars suggest that he began his tenure during the reign of Adad-nirari III.

Notably, the Antakya Stele, dating to the late 9th century BCE (807/06), references Samsi-ilu in the position of tartanu; however, due to Nergal-ilaya's identification as turtanu in the preceding year, it can be inferred that Samsi-ilu's career likely began after 808/07 BCE. Thus, it is reasonable to posit that Samsi-ilu's influence persisted for over half a century, highlighting the complexities of power dynamics within the Assyrian political landscape (Dearman & Graham, 2002, p. 137).

Scenario Analysis: The Political Dynamics of Nergal-ilaya and Shammuramat

In the historical context following the death of Shamsi-adad V, Nergal-ilaya emerged as a prominent figure, likely well acquainted with Shammu-ramat. The transitional period presented a unique opportunity for both parties to establish a mutually beneficial arrangement. If Shammu-ramat ascended to the role of Queen Regent with Nergal-ilaya's backing, she might appoint him as commander in chief, giving him extensive powers.

In this hypothetical scenario, he secures the title of commander in chief and becomes the eponymate during the second year of Shammu-ramat's regency, specifically in 829/28 BCE. After a twenty-one-year tenure as Queen Regent, during which she effectively governed, Shammu-ramat transitioned into the role of coregent with her son, Adad-nirari III, for an extended period.

When Adad-nirari III assumed kingship and the eponymic in 809/08 BCE,

Shammu-ramat's influence remained palpable. Concurrently, Nergal-ilaya, who had served as governor and commander in chief for four decades, faced the diminishing sands of time in his political career. It is improbable that either Shammu-ramat or Nergal-ilaya neglected to appoint a successor amenable to perpetuating the previously established near unrestricted use of power. His successor was Samsi-ilu.

Samsi-ilu, serving as the commander in chief of the Assyrian armed forces for at least half a century, appeared to function in a semi-autonomous capacity. He conducted military campaigns independently of the approval or permission of the monarchs under whom he served. He commissioned his own stelae to commemorate his achievements, often omitting any reference to the king.

The influence of Samsi-ilu waned towards the latter part of Ashur-nirari V's reign. The ascension of Tiglath-pileser III marked a significant shift, as he implemented reforms designed to curtail the power of high officials and governors. Furthermore, he endeavoured to dismantle the arrangements that had enabled Shammu-ramat to maintain her authority. Tiglath-pileser III probably sought to eradicate both the memory of Shammu-ramat and her legacy of empowered officials.

Tiglath-pileser III actively engaged in historical revisionism, systematically excising Shammu-ramat from the List of Kings and the Assyrian Eponym List, attempting to expropriate the records of his predecessors, and appropriating the accomplishments of others as his own. This behaviour exemplifies characteristics associated with narcissistic psychopathology, particularly manifesting as megalomania. The interplay of power dynamics, personal ambition, and the manipulation of collective memory significantly shapes the historical narrative during this period.

Who was King Pul?

The identity of King Pul, as referenced in biblical texts, remains a subject of scholarly debate. Pul appears in the Books of Kings and Chronicles during Menahem's reign in Israel. Many scholars identify Pul with Tiglath-pileser III, suggesting that the names refer to the same Assyrian ruler. This assertion overlooks the historical nuances surrounding the timelines of these figures. Tiglath-pileser III began his reign in 745/44 BCE, and historical records indicate that Menahem died around 750/49 BCE.

Despite strong support for the notion that Tiglath-pileser was a usurper, there is evidence suggesting their concurrent presence during the reign of Ashur-nirari V. A plausible hypothesis involves Tiglath-pileser's role as coregent with Ashur-nirari V for much of his reign. This association may explain why the Hebrew scribes later referred to him by his kingly title.

Tiglath-pileser III's annals document Menahem of Samaria and include references mistakenly dated to approximately 738/737 BCE. Thiele has significantly altered the sequence of the later kings of Israel to align with that date. In reality, these events occurred much earlier during Menahem's reign (761–751), when Tiglath-pileser served as coregent with Assur-nirari V, who is identified as either his father or brother.

Inscriptions from Ashur-nasir-pal articulate a profound fear of erasure and distortion of historical records, reflecting the political machinations prevalent among Assyrian kings. Such distortions have introduced significant challenges in understanding the Assyrian timeline and, by extension, its interactions with neighbouring nations. The Assyrian annals often reveal a tendency among kings to appropriate the victories and legacies of their predecessors, thereby reshaping historical narratives to serve contemporary political ends.

Many scholars in Assyriology acknowledge that several inscriptions attributed to Tiglath-pileser III refer to events preceding his reign. A fragmentary brick inscription identifies him as the son of Adad-nirari III; however, the Assyrian King List records him as the offspring of Ashur-nirari V (Pritchard, 1992, p. 556). The Assyrian archives yield scant information regarding Adad-nirari III and contain no references to Shalmaneser IV or Ashur-dan III. Significantly, an alabaster stele unearthed in 1894 at Tell Abta displays the name of Tiglath-pileser III superimposed over that of Shalmaneser IV, a direct successor to Adad-nirari III and the third sovereign preceding Tiglath-pileser III (Grayson, 1999).

Many scholars convincingly argue that Tiglath-pileser III intentionally appropriated the achievements of his predecessors, including Adad-nirari III. However, it is also reasonable to propose that he omitted references to earlier rulers whose accomplishments could have overshadowed his own. Such actions align with the pattern of behavior historically associated with Tiglath-pileser III.

Notably, the reign preceding that of Adad-nirari III, attributed to Shammu-ramat, was characterized by the unprecedented consolidation of power among high officials during her tenure as Queen Regent and subsequently in a less prominent role. The legacy of Shammu-ramat, also known as Semiramis, is well documented across the historical accounts of neighbouring nations, which frequently highlight her name and deeds.

Moreover, her stele at Usshur affirms her status as an official limmu; however, the official annals have systematically excised her legacy and eponyms from the time of her reign. This text aims to contribute to the rectification of this significant gap in historical understanding. The prevailing scholarly consensus suggests that Shammu-ramat served as Queen Regent for a duration that some estimate as three years. However, a more comprehensive examination of the available evidence indicates the necessity for a period extending to twenty-one years.

CHAPTER 11

Sennacherib's contribution:

The Taylor Prism records the 8 campaigns of Tiglath-pileser III

Sennacherib's documentation of his military campaigns represents a notable departure from the traditional chronological recording practices of his predecessor, Sargon II. In the 1840s, archaeological discoveries at Sargon II's "Palace without Rival" site in Khorsabad unveiled numerous inscriptions that detailed Sargon's campaigns, systematically organized according to the years of his reign. In contrast, Sennacherib adopted a numerical approach to chronicle his campaigns, eschewing a direct correlation with the years of his rule.

A significant aspect of Sennacherib's recording method involved creating multiple baked clay "prisms," specifically six-sided prisms, which served to disseminate his accomplishments. Currently, four nearly identical complete prisms, along with various fragments housed in the British Museum, are extant. The inaugural prism, identified as the Taylor Prism, was unearthed in Nineveh in 1830 by Colonel Robert Taylor. The Oriental Institute Prism, the Jerusalem Prism, and the Sennacherib Prism are notable examples; the Sennacherib Prism was acquired from an antiquities dealer in 1919. Each prism measures approximately 38 cm (16 in.) in height and 14 cm (5½ in.) in width.

Despite their relatively modest dimensions, these artifacts encompass a substantial wealth of information that has proven instrumental in uncovering historical truths. Notably, research indicates that the campaigns documented by Sennacherib correspond to significant events recorded by Sargon, suggesting that Sargon and

Sennacherib served as coregents for a considerable duration of Sargon's reign, if not its entirety. As noted by Radner (2012), "Sargon was already middle-aged when he came to power: he must have been at least forty years old and had at least one adult son, Sennacherib, who from the start of his father's reign assisted him in running the empire as crown prince."

This collaborative governance underscores the complexity of their familial and political dynamics within the Assyrian imperial structure.

Comparing the records of Sargon II and Sennacherib:

Sargon II – Year 1	**Sennacherib – First Campaign**
Sargon went against ***Merodach-baladan***, the ruler of Babylon, whose reign began at the same time as Sargon's. He states that during that year, "On the ***Tu'munu*** tribe I imposed Assur's yoke".	"In my first campaign I accomplished the defeat of ***Merodach-baladan***, king of Babylonia, together with the army of Elam, his ally, in the plain of Kish ....On my return (march), the ***Tu'muna*** ... not submissive ... I conquered."

Sargon II -Year 8	**Sennacherib's Second Campaign**
*"In my eighth year of reign I went against the lands of the ...**Medes** .... I carried off their spoil".*	*"In my second campaign, Assur my lord, encouraged me, and .... On my return, I received the heavy tribute of the distant **Medes**, whose name no one among the kings, my fathers, had (ever) heard."*

When the Assyrians first encountered the Medes, the situation remains complex, particularly in light of Sargon II's documentation of military campaigns against them purportedly more than a decade earlier. A plausible explanation emerges when considering that Sargon II's campaign in his eighth year correlates with Sennacherib's second military expedition.

Notably, Sennacherib's professed lack of awareness regarding the Medes is perplexing, especially given that references to the Medes appeared in the annals of Shalmaneser III approximately a century and a half earlier. Furthermore, the biblical account in 2 Kings 17:6 indicates that numerous Samaritans were transported to "the cities of the Medes" during the reign of Shalmaneser V, adding another layer of complexity to the historical narrative surrounding Assyrian-Median interactions.

Sargon II – Years 9 to 11	Sennacherib's Third Campaign
Sargon of Assyria played a significant role in the early stages of the military campaign, culminating in the Jerusalem siege. The biblical account in Isaiah 20:1 shows this involvement: "In the year that Tartan came to Ashdod, Sargon, the king of Assyria, sent him to fight against Ashdod and took it." Furthermore, the term "tartan," as referenced in 2 Kings 18:17, pertains to the Assyrian commander dispatched to confront King Hezekiah at Jerusalem, operating under the authority of his coregent, Sennacherib. Notably, the specific name of the tartan during this period was Inurta-Ilaya.	In Sennacherib's third campaign, between 716 and 714 BCE, he targeted Hittite territories in Syria and confronted King Hezekiah of Judah. He besieged 46 fortified cities and depicted Hezekiah as a "caged bird" within Jerusalem, which he referred to as a "caged city." To strengthen his siege, Sennacherib built extensive earthworks and allegedly redirected the city's water supply to increase suffering among its inhabitants.

Sargon II -Year 12	Sennacherib's Fourth Campaign
"In my twelfth year of reign, ***Merodach-baladan***, ... violated the oath and curse (invoked in the name of) the great gods, and withheld his tribute. .... ***Humbanigash, the Elamite***, came to his aid. ....The might of Assur ... and Marduk, which I had made to prevail against those cities .... ***Babylon***, the city of the lords, I entered amidst rejoicing ...."	"In my fourth campaign .... ***Merodach-baladan***, whose defeat I had brought about in the course of my first campaign, and whose forces I had shattered ... his cities I destroyed, I devastated, I made like ruin heaps. Upon his ally, ***the king of Elam***, I poured out terror ..... On my return I placed on [***Babylon***'s] royal throne, Assur-nâdin-shum, my oldest son, ... I made subject to him the wide land of Sumer and Akkad."

Sennacherib's Fifth Campaign:

Sennacherib's fifth military campaign around 709/708 BC targeted the areas northeast of Nineveh, particularly near Mount Judi. This campaign is not mentioned in Sargon II's inscriptions, hinting that Sargon considered this campaign to be of minor importance. However, it was apparently of some significance for Sennacherib.

Sargon II – Year 13	Sennacherib's Sixth Campaign
"Dûr-Iakini, his stronghold, *I burned with fire*; its high defences *I destroyed, I devastated*; ... *I made it like a mound* left by the flood. The people of Sippar, Nippur, **Babylon**, Borsippa, who were imprisoned therein through no fault of theirs, - I broke their bonds and caused them to behold the light (of day). ....I waged bitter warfare against *the people of Elam.... people from Bît-Iakin* [which my hands had conquered], I settled [in Calah] ...."	"The cities which were in those provinces *I destroyed, I devastated, I burned with fire. To mounds and ruins* I turned (them). On my return march Shuzubu, *the Babylonian*, who during an uprising in the land had turned to himself the rule of Sumer and Akkad .... I accomplished his defeat in a battle ....*The king of Elam* .... His forces I scattered and I shattered his host.... *the people of Bît-Iakin* ... not a rebel (lit., sinner) escaped. I had them ... on the way to Assyria.

Sargon II – Year 15	Sennacherib's Seventh Campaign
".... *Shuturnahundu, the Elamite*. [He lent his aid and came] to [the king of Ellipi's] rescue. .... Seven of my officials, governors, I sent .... 4,500 Elamite bowmen, fled to save their lives and went up into the city of Marubishti. .... Him, together with his fighters they	"*The Elamite, Kudur-nahundu*, heard of the overthrow of his cities, terror overwhelmed him, the (people of) the rest of his cities he brought into the strongholds. He himself left Madaktu, his royal city, and took his way to the city of Haidala, which is in the

brought in bonds and fetters before me .... Over all [of Elam] ... people of Ellipi, to the farthest border, I caused to dwell in habitations of peace, my royal yoke [I placed upon them], and they were subject to me."	distant mountains. .... Kudur-Nahundu, the king of Elam, did not live three months longer ... but died suddenly, before his appointed time. After him, Umman-menanu ... his younger (?) brother, sat on his throne."
Sargon II – Year 17 "In the seventeenth year [the Assyrian king] ... came to Ecbatana [i.e. **Babylon**], captured its towers, plundered its markets, and turned its glory into disgrace….. Then he returned to Nineveh, he and all his combined forces, a vast body of troops; and there he and his forces ***rested and feasted*** for one hundred and twenty days."	**Sennacherib's Eighth Campaign** "I advanced swiftly against ***Babylon*** .... Like the on-coming of a storm I broke loose .... I completely invested that city, with mines and engines .... The plunder .... with the princes of (all) countries, the governors of my land ... nobles, officials ... of Assyria, I took up my abode in that palace and instituted ***a feast of music***.

Conclusions:

Crucially, these records align chronologically and reflect consistent geographical locations and key individuals involved in the events described. The statistical likelihood of such congruities occurring purely by chance is exceedingly low.

Therefore, the most reasonable deduction is that both records pertain to the same events. We can propose that Sennacherib's Third Campaign did not take place in the traditionally accepted year of 701 BCE; instead, it should be adjusted to 715/714 BCE. This re-evaluation challenges us to reconsider historical narratives that may rely on assumptions and scholarship lacking rigor.

Further evidence for the coregency between Sargon II and Sennacherib:

Sargon II and Sennacherib as depicted in Sennacherib's Palace

Evidence from Sargon II's Palace at Khorsabad

The king is distinctly recognizable in the relief due to his tiara and scepter as he faces the crown prince. In Assyrian and Babylonian artistic conventions, the crown prince is invariably depicted on panels or stelae at a height equal to that of the king, adorned with a diadem featuring two ribbons trailing behind his head. He consistently faces the king, who, in addition to wearing a tiara (Reade, 2009: 252–254), also displays the same two ribbons at the back of his head.

The identification of these two figures is unambiguous, as the art of the Assyrian and Babylonian periods adheres to a stereotypical hierarchy in which gods, kings, and their subjects are represented according to size. This hierarchical representation establishes that when a character adjacent to a king is depicted at an equal stature and adorned with a tiara, that character is another king. Conversely, if the character is depicted without a tiara but still in possession of regalia, this suggests the status of a coregent (Pritchard, 1969: 159, 199, 351).

King Sargon II and his coregent, King Sennacherib, are the two dignitaries under consideration. Various depictions and inscriptions at Khorsabad corroborate these identities, further establishing that they were distinct individuals rather than the same person.

Moreover, their status as coregents is critical to understanding their roles in the Assyrian monarchy. In Jewish tradition, Sennacherib is acknowledged as a coregent, referred to by the Hebrews as King Sennacherib. Consequently, Sennacherib held the title of King during the siege of Jerusalem in 715/714 BCE.

Resetting Landmark Dates

This book elucidates previously elusive absolute dates within the context of the Hebrew Scriptures, which, while addressing religious and spiritual themes, also serve as an invaluable repository of historical data. Through meticulous analysis, we have constructed a comprehensive timeline that critically engages with established narratives, providing a wealth of information. Instead of creating a chimera by conflating Hebrew and Assyrian histories, this study reconciles over seventy data points from the Books of Kings and Chronicles. This research culminates in a detailed chart representing the entire Divided Kingdom period. We undertook a comparative analysis of Hebrew and Assyrian records only after this systematic reconciliation, thereby identifying discrepancies within the Assyrian historical accounts.

The revised Hebrew chronology demonstrates a notable alignment with the Assyrian timeline, extending back only to approximately 800 BCE. The occurrence of the total solar eclipse in 763 BCE serves as a critical reference point, corroborating the ninth year of Ashur-dan III. Decades prior to this juncture, a discernible gap of twenty-one years manifests, evidenced by the irregularities in the pattern of eponyms following the death of Shamsi-Adad V. This discontinuity in the historical record appears to be addressed by the reign of Shammu-ramat, whose historical accounts seem to have been systematically purged, presumably under the influence of Tiglath Pileser III.

The discrepancy of twenty-one years prevails in all dates before 800 BCE and may explain the twenty to thirty-year variations in Egyptian dates quoted as far back as the Middle Kingdom. Although dates attributed to the Battle of Qarqar (853 BCE) and the events recorded on the Black Obelisk (841 BCE) have been accepted as solid, the reconciliation of the Hebrew data casts doubt on those dates.

The implications of the Hebrew timeline calculations are of considerable significance, as they challenge the foundational assumptions prevalent in Assyriology and ancient historical studies. Based on the principles of the scientific method, the assertions presented in this discourse warrant thorough scrutiny and critical examination. The chronologies in more recent periods closely align with established consensus; however, academic scrutiny will focus on the earlier dates, especially the chronological marker for the inception of the Divided Kingdom, denoted as 952 BCE.

Confirming the 952 BCE Date

One notable characteristic of the Hebrew Scriptures is their tendency to document extensive intervals between significant historical events. Among these, there are four particularly noteworthy chronological records. One such record establishes a fascinating chronological connection between the date of the Exodus and an event that occurred during the reign of King Solomon. This period immediately precedes the establishment of the Divided Kingdom.

The pertinent reference is found in 1 Kings 6:1, which states: "And it came to pass in the four hundred and eightieth year after the children of Israel were come out of the land of Egypt, in the fourth year of Solomon's reign over Israel, in the month Zif, which is the second month, that he began to build the house of the Lord" (KJV). This verse shows the timeline of important events in Israelite history.

The Building of Solomon's Temple

The traditional argument for dating the building of Solomon's Temple involves historical records by Menander of Ephesus, a second-century BCE historian. Josephus used his work on Tyre, now lost.

Three independent sources confirm the timeline for Menander's list of Tyrian kings, including Baal-Eser II. Two of these sources relate to biblical events: Hiram's assistance to Solomon and an Assyrian record of tribute paid by Baal-Eser II to Shalmaneser III.

Baal-Eser II, also known as Balbazer II, was a Tyrian king. He was the son of Ithobaal I and brother of Jezebel. Josephus mentions him as having reigned for six years, although Eusebius states it was eighteen years. Tyre was very influential during his reign, with his sister as queen of Israel and his niece Athaliah as queen of Judah.

Tyre did not oppose Shalmaneser III at the Battle of Qarqar, but Baal-Eser II paid tribute to him twelve years later. Jehu of Israel also paid tribute during this time. This tribute helped revise the timelines of Baal-Eser's successors, Mattan I and Pygmalion, pushing their reigns back by eleven years from the traditionally accepted dates.

The Pervasiveness of the Assyrian Timeline

The dates for Baal-Eser II's reign have been generally accepted as 846 to 841 BCE. His final year of reign corresponded to his payment of tribute to Shalmaneser III, as recorded on the Kurkh Monolith.

The calculations in this book reveal a twenty-one-year gap in the Assyrian timeline, indicating that the events recorded on the Monolith occurred in 862 BCE rather than 841 BCE. This correction means that all dates in the Tyrian King List for the kings are shifted twenty-one years earlier. Hiram I, for example, reigned from 980 to 947 BCE, but with this adjustment, his reign is revised to 1001 to 968 BCE. Consequently, the construction of Solomon's Temple aligns closely with these calculations, establishing 989 BCE as the correct date. This error in the Assyrian timeline has significant implications for dating Assyria's interactions with surrounding nations.

Establishing the Absolute Date for the Exodus

The chronology of Solomon's Temple necessitates a nuanced analysis that transcends the simplistic arithmetic approach of subtracting four hundred and eighty years. By aligning the commencement of Rehoboam's reign with 1 Nisan 952 BCE, we can anchor Solomon's forty-year reign to this pivotal date, beginning 1 Nisan 992 BCE. Historical evidence indicates that Solomon passed away in late 953 or early 952 BCE; however, conventional historiography credits him with the entirety of his final regnal year. These calculations establish that Solomon's fourth year spans from 1 Nisan 989 to 29 Adar 988 BCE.

Within the scriptural canon, the second month is designated as Zif, corresponding to the contemporary month of Iyar. Thus, the commencement of Solomon's Temple construction occurred in Iyar of 989 BCE.

The reference to the four hundred and eightieth year implies a period exceeding

479 years but remaining less than 480. This observation is significant, as the resultant date must align precisely with the fourteenth day of the first month, Nisan, as articulated in Exodus 12. Hence, the calculated date of 14 Nisan 1468 BCE emerges as a critical temporal marker, representing 479 years and one month prior to the onset of Temple construction.

Verifying the Exodus date through Egyptian records presents a complex challenge, particularly in correlating it with the established date of Solomon's Temple construction, 989 BCE. Determining the Exodus date does not automatically affirm the proposed timeline unless it is substantiated by synchronisms within the Egyptian historical corpus.

The discourse surrounding the Exodus is further complicated by three predominant chronological frameworks: High Chronology, Middle Chronology, and Low Chronology. Each framework offers different perspectives on the timing of ancient events, necessitating rigorous analysis to achieve a reliable synchronism with Egyptian records.

If the proposed date of 1468 BCE aligns with any established chronological model, it would provide substantial support for that timeline, enhancing its credibility within historical scholarship. Notably, Egyptian historical narratives include precedents where significant events correspond with celestial observations, suggesting that such alignments may reinforce the broader context of historical analysis.

Ancient Egyptian records detail various celestial events, primarily used for calendars, temple construction, and religious rituals. Among these, the heliacal rising of Sirius signaled the New Year and was essential for predicting the annual flooding of the Nile.

Events in Egyptian History Corresponding to Celestial Events

The uninterrupted historical narrative of ancient Egypt, extending back to approximately 3000 BCE, underscores the importance of celestial observations in societal practices. However, such observations are sparsely documented within the extensive corpus of inscriptions. Yet, the unique contribution of one of the two primary inscriptions in providing chronological markers for the timeframe under examination cannot be overstated.

Example 1: In the ninth year of Amenhotep I's reign, observers meticulously recorded the heliacal rising of Sothis on the ninth day of the third month of the summer season. Contemporary astronomers have concluded that if observed from Memphis or Heliopolis, the event corresponds to 1537 BCE according to the New Kingdom High Chronology. If observed from Thebes, it dates to 1517 BCE, following the New Kingdom Low Chronology. Helck, Wolfgang; Otto, Eberhard; and Drenkhahn, Rosmarie corroborated this in their 1975 publication. While providing a historical reference, this information is insufficient for precise chronological refinement.

Example 2: The year 1468 BCE falls within the reign of Pharaoh Thutmose III, consistent across both High and Low Chronology frameworks. Notably, the Battle of Megiddo is recorded during this period. Thutmose III's Hall of Annals at the Temple of Amun in Karnak states that the battle occurred on "Year 23, I Shemu [day] 21, the exact day of the feast of the new moon," indicating a lunar date (Urk. 18:657.2). "Year 23" refers to the twenty-third year of Thutmose's reign.

Given the cyclical nature of the lunar calendar, this Egyptian date corresponds to the New Moon approximately every twenty-five years, facilitating alignment of the historical battle date with known lunar cycles. Scholars including von Beckerath, Krauss, Barta, Hornung, and Murnane argue that the Battle of Megiddo likely occurred on 16 April 1457 BCE, within the twenty-third year of Thutmose III's reign, which they approximate began in 1479 BCE. However, even meticulous calculations remain contingent on variables not always considered in the original assessments.

Upon initial examination, labeling 1479 BCE as the beginning of Thutmose III's reign presents several challenges. As the Pharaoh linked to the Exodus narrative, he needed to possess:

1. The requisite maturity and authority to engage with Moses during the repeated entreaties to "Let my people go";

2. The capacity to have fathered an offspring who would succumb during the occurrence of the tenth plague; and

3. Direct command over the military forces deployed in pursuit of the departing Hebrews.

These factors raise significant questions that demand a deeper analysis to understand the chronological accuracy of Thutmose III's accession date.

Impediments to Accepting the 1479 BCE Date

In the 1479 BCE scenario, Thutmose III was merely two years old. By the proposed date of the Exodus in 1468 BCE, he would have been thirteen, an age at which he would likely not possess the requisite attributes to govern effectively or to have fathered a child, as discussed in preceding sections. Following the premature death of his father, Thutmose II, after a reign of only three years, his stepmother, Hatshepsut, initially held the position of Regent and subsequently governed as Pharaoh from approximately the seventh year of Thutmose III's accession until her death during her twenty-second year. While some scholars have posited that the Pharaoh during the Exodus could have been Hatshepsut, a notable female ruler, the biblical narrative consistently represents the Pharaoh in a male context.

Throughout the biblical account of the Exodus, the Pharaoh is uniformly depicted using masculine pronouns and terminology. This consistent portrayal reinforces the established perception of the Pharaoh as a male figure within the text, aligning with traditional interpretations of this historical narrative.

The High Chronology Date for Thutmose III's Reign (1504 – 1450 BCE)

Edward Wente, a respected Professor Emeritus of Egyptology, has conducted extensive research on the formalities and preparatory processes involved in ancient Egyptian rituals. In his scholarly analysis, he highlighted May 16, 1482, the date of the Battle of Megiddo, as a significant point of interest warranting further investigation. Additionally, Wente proposes that the year 1504 should be recognized as the accession year for Thutmose III, in line with the High Chronology. He discusses this topic in his article, "Accession and the Beginning of the New Kingdom," published in the Journal of Near Eastern Studies, Volume 34, Issue 4, in October 1975, on pages 265 to 272. Other notable Egyptologists support this perspective, contributing to ongoing debates surrounding competing timelines in the field.

Possible Synchronisms Resulting from the 1504 BCE Date

Amenemhat, the designated heir of Pharaoh Thutmose III, is a notable figure in ancient Egyptian history. As the son of Thutmose III and Queen Satiah, his lineage held considerable significance. Historical records indicate that Thutmose III named Amenemhat the "king's eldest son." In the twenty-fourth year of Thutmose's reign, Amenemhat also held the title of "Overseer of the Cattle of Amun." Historians believe that Queen Satiah died around this time, while reports indicate that Prince Amenemhat passed away approximately in the thirty-fifth year of Thutmose III's reign.

The demise of the Pharaoh's eldest son bears a significant correlation with the biblical narrative in the Book of Exodus. The text articulates, "And it came to pass, that at midnight the Lord smote all the firstborn in the land of Egypt, from the firstborn of Pharaoh that sat on his throne unto the firstborn of the captive that was in the dungeon; and all the firstborn of cattle" (Exodus 12:29). Importantly, the thirty-fifth year of Thutmose III's reign is historically recorded as 1469 BCE (High Chronology), which closely aligns with the calculated date of the Exodus, proposed as 1468 BCE in this analysis. This timing may provide a historical basis for the biblical story within ancient Egyptian history, a connection of considerable significance.

Thutmose III's Tenth Campaign in His Thirty-Fifth Year

Another issue reflected in the Egyptian records is the destruction of the Egyptian army, or at least its elite divisions. Of all the Pharaohs, Thutmose III's military campaigns are the most comprehensively documented, with at least seventeen recorded. The records pertaining to his tenth military campaign reflect a period of intense conflict. In the thirty-fifth year of his reign, the king of Mitanni assembled a substantial military contingent and engaged the Egyptian forces near Aleppo. Consistent with traditional practices, Thutmose proclaimed a decisive victory following the encounter.

Nevertheless, the limited quantity of spoils retrieved from this engagement prompts a critical examination of the veracity of his claims. The annals inscribed at Karnak indicate that Thutmose captured only ten prisoners of war, implying that the outcome of the confrontation may have been markedly less favorable than officially reported.

After completing his arduous tenth military campaign, the Pharaoh returned to Egypt following the fighting season of 1469 BCE. Egypt, primarily an agricultural society, did not maintain a standing army. The lack of full-time military personnel meant commanders had to conduct campaigns when the labor demand in the fields was lower. Upon his return, Pharaoh Thutmose focused on domestic matters.

Moses, a Hebrew raised in the Pharaoh's court with a unique relationship to the royal family, implored the Pharaoh to "let my people go."

According to biblical accounts, each refusal by the Pharaoh was met with supernatural retribution, culminating in the well-documented Ten Plagues of Egypt, as recounted in the Torah. These events transpired over a protracted timeframe, extending several months. The final plague involved the smiting of the firstborn in the land, a tragedy that notably included the Pharaoh's son, Amenemhat, who would have been in his late teenage years at that time. This significant event occurred on 14 Nisan 1468 BCE, marking a pivotal moment in the historical and religious narrative of the Hebrew people. Their departure at the dramatic hour of midnight, heading towards the promised land, invokes a sense of anticipation.

A Reexamination of the Established Historical Narrative

The dominant scholarly narrative suggests that Thutmose III entered into matrimony with the non-royal Merytre-Hatshepsut following the death of Amenemhat, a strategic alliance ostensibly designed to ensure the production of a male heir. Upon his father's death in 1450 BCE, Amenhotep II assumed the throne at eighteen, leading scholars to estimate his birth around 1468 BCE, indicating that his conception likely occurred in the preceding year. This chronology exposes a notable incongruity within the posited historical framework.

Significantly, according to High Chronology, it is believed that Amenhotep II's wife, Satiah, passed away circa 1480 BCE. This date coincides with Amenemhat's appointment as "Overseer of the Cattle of Amun." It seems improbable that any Pharaoh would have allowed a protracted interval exceeding a decade before acquiring a queen or consort, barring substantial rationale. The occurrences during Thutmose III's twenty-fourth regnal year may have reinforced the Pharaoh's commitment to preparing his heir for future governance.

As Amenemhat approached age twenty, he would likely have sought a bride, though there is no surviving documentation of this event. With the succession of his son seemingly assured, Thutmose III may have opted to seek a new queen. Historical records further indicate that, in addition to Satiah and Merytre-Hatshepsut, Thutmose III partook in several subsequent marriages, notably to women such as Nebtu, Menwi, Merti, Menhet, and Nebsemi. Three of these unions were likely diplomatic, with foreign wives wed to Thutmose to secure valuable political alliances.

A Cause to Take Pause

The evidence suggests a significant connection between Amenhotep's birth and Amenemhat's death, with speculation that Amenhotep was born just before Amenemhat died. In the biblical narrative, Pharaoh hardened his heart, and God intervened to harden Pharaoh's heart multiple times. This ongoing stubbornness eventually led to the tenth plague, which tragically resulted in the death of Pharaoh's firstborn son. An intriguing question arises: did the God of the Hebrews intentionally ensure that Pharaoh received a replacement heir even before enacting judgment? This book is primarily centered on the exploration of mathematical relationships, with attention devoted to maintaining focus and avoiding deviations from the core subject matter. However, certain mathematical concepts may inadvertently give rise to speculative discussions.

The Loss of the Egyptian Army

The biblical narrative famously describes an event in which the Egyptian army was overwhelmed by the sea while pursuing the Hebrews following their miraculous crossing. While skeptics may dismiss this account as a fable, it is important to recognize an undeniable historical fact: there was a significant decline in the Egyptian military's ability to conduct extensive campaigns following the thirty-fifth year of Thutmose III's reign. This decline warrants thorough examination within the context of historical events and their interpretations.

"In later campaigns, Thutmose III was content to consolidate what he had won and to lay the foundations of an imperial organization of his Asian possessions. Native rulers, members of local ruling dynasties, were henceforward set to govern their own territories as vassals of Egypt and were bound by solemn oath to keep the peace, render annual tribute, and obey the Egyptian representative in the region, the overseer of foreign lands. Their sons were sent as hostages to Egypt and educated at court, so that in due course they might return to rule their inheritance, Egyptianized in outlook and sympathies." (Britannica)

His final significant military campaign occurred in his thirty-fifth year, during which he engaged the Mittani. In his forty-second year, he once again confronted the persistent challenges posed by the Mittani, achieving only partial success in this endeavor.

In Conclusion

The precision of the interlocking data will strike any mathematician examining how the figures for the Divided Kingdom converge. The 230 years from 952 to 722 BCE define a framework of thirty-four cross-references that tightly connect the reigns of nineteen kings of Israel and thirteen kings of Judah. There is no comparable example in ancient history that offers this level of chronological detail. The keys to uncovering the secrets of the mysterious numbers have remained hidden until now. The solution does not lie in some long-lost code. Research reveals that conservative assumptions apply, including the understanding that the New Year of Kings is offset by six months between the Kingdoms of Israel and Judah, and that the Mishnah was correct when it described the accounting of reigns according to the post-dating system.

One piece of evidence for the accuracy of this timeline is the calculation connected to the fourth year of Solomon's reign, specifically the mention of the 480th year in 1 Kings 6:1. This brings us back to 1468 BCE, the year of the Exodus. Notably, this year corresponds to the thirty-fifth year of Pharaoh Thutmose III's reign. Historians recognize this year as significant in Thutmose III's reign because it marked the death of his son and was also the year he had to pause his major military campaigns, opting instead for missions that were far less ambitious.

The meticulous observance and recording of chronological details seem to be a hallmark of Hebrew scholarship. The Hebrews maintained a highly reliable system for documenting dates and spans of time. By reconciling the data from the books of Kings and Chronicles, we can gain valuable insights into the timelines of nations that interacted with Judah and Israel. Historians and archaeologists will greatly benefit from this information in their respective fields of study.

Several significant time periods are noted in the Hebrew texts. One such period is the 430 years mentioned in Exodus 12:40-41. Verse 40 states, "Now the sojourning of the children of Israel who dwelt in Egypt was four hundred and thirty years." The Septuagint provides additional clarification by expanding the phrase "who dwelt in Egypt" to "who dwelt in Egypt and Canaan." Many researchers agree that the time from when Jacob and his family settled in Egypt until the Exodus was likely no more than 215 years.

The 430-year period begins in the year Abram, later known as Abraham, left Ur and entered Canaan at the age of seventy-five. To determine the start date, we calculate 430 years before 1468 BCE, which brings us to 1898 BCE. Subtracting seventy-five years from that, we arrive at 1973 BCE, marking the birth of Abram. Chronologists base these calculations on the peculiarities of various calendars that might have been in use.

The average length of a year in the Hebrew luni-solar calendar aligns closely with a Julian year. However, before 1644 BCE, the Hebrews utilized a schematic calendar consisting of 360 days, in addition to an agrarian calendar to plan sowing and harvesting. The use of the 360-day calendar means that seventy years in this system is nearly equivalent to sixty-nine Julian years.

For followers of Abrahamic faiths—Judaism, Christianity, and Islam—scholars revised Abraham's birth year to 1968 BCE and determined that he arrived in Canaan in 1894 BCE. These calculations are made possible by achieving an absolute timeline for the Divided Kingdom. The potential for unraveling many ancient timelines is nearly limitless.

John Ferris

About the Author

John P. Ferris, born in 1955, is semi-retired and resides just south of Brisbane, Australia. He is currently active in his local church, focusing on Pastoral Care. Throughout his career, he managed various roles in real estate, the automotive industry, finance, franchising, and transportation.

John has always had a passion for helping people and is involved in charitable efforts in southern India, where he focuses on assisting the poor, widows, and orphans. Cooking is another of his passions, and his specialty dishes, particularly his slow-cooked brisket, are well-received by the homeless and disadvantaged.

As well as an intense interest in the mathematics of the Bible, John has a collection of poems to his credit, some of which he recites on occasion.

www.ingramcontent.com/pod-product-compliance
Lightning Source LLC
Chambersburg PA
CBHW041114120626
46547CB00019B/2705